Success Strategies of the World Most Successful men and how to Apply them in Your Life

GORDON MILLS

Published by BEATRICE, 2023.

While every precaution has been taken in the preparation of this book, the publisher assumes no responsibility for errors or omissions, or for damages resulting from the use of the information contained herein.

SUCCESS STRATEGIES OF THE WORLD MOST SUCCESSFUL MEN AND HOW TO APPLY THEM IN YOUR LIFE

First edition. July 6, 2023.

Copyright © 2023 GORDON MILLS.

ISBN: 979-8223047827

Written by GORDON MILLS.

Also by GORDON MILLS

5 Ways to Become Mysterious

Building Generational Wealth : Unveiling the Secrets of Long-Term Financial Prosperity

The 5 Rules of Billionaires

The 4 Strategic Secrets of Success : Unlocking Your Success Blueprint - Secrets to Extraordinary Achievement

The 5 Rules of Money : The Golden Rules of Making and Increasing Money

The 7cs of Success : Confidence, Consistency, Conception, Concentration, Character, Commitment and Capacity to Enjoy

Success Strategies of the World Most Successful men and how to Apply them in Your Life

SUCCESS STRATEGIES OF THE WORLD MOST SUCCESSFUL MEN AND HOW TO APPLY THEM IN YOUR LIFE

Your Ultimate Encyclopedia to Financial Freedom Now!

GORDON MILLS

Copyright@GordonMills2023

Introduction

Are you ready to unlock the secrets of success from some of the world's most accomplished individuals? Imagine gaining access to the proven strategies and insights that have propelled the likes of Bill Gates, Elon Musk, Robert Kiyosaki, Warren Buffett, Steve Jobs, and Mark Zuckerberg to the pinnacle of achievement. These visionary titans have not only revolutionized industries but also transformed the way we perceive success itself.

In this captivating book, we delve into the success strategies of these extraordinary individuals, dissecting their philosophies and distilling their wisdom into actionable steps that you can apply in your own life. Each of these exceptional men has left an indelible mark on their respective fields, and by learning from their experiences, you have the opportunity to unlock your true potential and embark on a transformative journey towards unparalleled success.

Discover how Bill Gates, the tech magnate and co-founder of Microsoft, exemplifies the value of relentless determination, strategic thinking, and embracing opportunities. Discover how Elon Musk, the visionary entrepreneur behind SpaceX and Tesla, challenges the status quo, takes audacious risks, and inspires innovation that transcends boundaries.

Unearth the investment principles of Robert Kiyosaki, renowned for his insights on financial intelligence and wealth creation. Delve into the strategies of Warren Buffett, the legendary investor and business tycoon, as he emphasizes the power of patience, value-based investing, and the ability to think long-term.

Immerse yourself in the philosophy of Steve Jobs, the iconic co-founder of Apple, who advocated for following your passion, relentless focus, and perfection in design. Uncover the lessons from Mark Zuckerberg, the creator of Facebook, who encourages embracing risks, staying focused amidst criticism, and fostering innovation in a rapidly evolving world.

But this book is not limited to simply admiring their accomplishments from afar. We go beyond the surface to distill their success strategies into actionable steps that you can apply in your own life. Whether you aspire to become an entrepreneur, investor, or leader in your chosen field, this comprehensive guide equips you with the tools, mindset, and strategies to turn your dreams into reality.

Get ready to embark on a transformative journey as we unveil the success strategies of these remarkable individuals and equip you with the insights, inspiration, and practical steps to incorporate their wisdom into your own life. It's time to unleash your full potential, defy limitations, and redefine what success means to you. Get ready to embrace the success strategies of the world's most accomplished men and embark on an extraordinary path to personal and professional greatness.

Chapter 1: Bill Gates' 7 Rules of Success

BILL GATES, THE RENOWNED American business magnate, software developer, and philanthropist, has left an indelible mark on the world. As the co-founder of Microsoft, Gates revolutionized the technology industry, becoming one of the richest individuals and an influential figure in the realm of global development. While his contributions to technology and philanthropy are widely recognized, Gates' success can be attributed not only to his intellect and innovation but also to the principles he abides by.

Throughout his illustrious career, Bill Gates has shared invaluable insights into his approach to success and the philosophies that have guided him. By distilling his experiences and observations, Gates has outlined seven key principles that can serve as a roadmap for achievement and personal growth. These principles, known as "Bill Gates' 7 Rules of Success," have inspired countless individuals across the globe, transcending the boundaries of the business world.

In this book, we will discover each of these rules in detail, delving into the wisdom they offer and the impact they can have on one's journey towards success. Whether you aspire to make a difference in the world of technology, entrepreneurship, or any other field, Gates' rules can provide you with valuable insights and guidance.

Gates emphasizes the importance of pursuing your passions and nurturing a curious mindset. By embracing curiosity, one opens doors to new ideas and opportunities that fuel innovation and growth.

Gates stresses the significance of setting clear, achievable goals and maintaining unwavering focus. This discipline helps channel efforts effectively, ensuring progress towards long-term objectives.

Building a strong and diverse network of individuals who share your vision and values is vital for success. Gates emphasizes the power of collaboration and learning from others' expertise and experiences.

Continuous learning and intellectual curiosity are central to Gates' philosophy. In a rapidly evolving world, he encourages individuals to embrace lifelong learning, adapt to change, and stay ahead of the curve.

Gates views failure not as a setback but as an opportunity for growth. By embracing failure, analyzing mistakes, and learning from them, one can develop resilience and ultimately achieve success.

Gates advocates for embracing innovation and thinking beyond conventional boundaries. By fostering a culture of innovation, individuals can disrupt industries, drive progress, and make a lasting impact.

Gates' philanthropic endeavors are well-known, and he emphasizes the importance of giving back to society. By using success as a platform for positive change, one can leave a lasting legacy and contribute to the greater good.

Bill Gates' 7 Rules of Success offer timeless wisdom that transcends the realm of technology and entrepreneurship. These principles provide a guiding light for anyone seeking personal and professional growth, igniting the spark needed to overcome challenges and make a lasting impact on the world.

Work Hard, No Excuses

In the pursuit of success, one of the core principles that has defined Bill Gates' journey is encapsulated in his simple yet powerful mantra: "Work Hard, No Excuses." This resolute philosophy has been instrumental in shaping Gates' illustrious career and serves as an enduring reminder of the dedication and commitment required to achieve extraordinary accomplishments.

Bill Gates, the co-founder of Microsoft and a prominent figure in the technology industry, embodies the notion that hard work forms the foundation of achievement. His remarkable ascent from a young entrepreneur to one of the world's wealthiest individuals stands as a testament to the transformative power of a strong work ethic.

Gates firmly believes that success is not merely a product of talent or luck but a result of consistent effort, perseverance, and a refusal to make excuses. By internalizing this mindset, individuals can unlock their true potential and overcome the obstacles that inevitably arise along their paths.

In this book, we delve deeper into the significance of Gates' mantra, exploring the underlying principles it embodies and the impact it can have on personal and professional growth.

A Commitment to Excellence:

Gates' "Work Hard, No Excuses" philosophy centers around the relentless pursuit of excellence. It requires individuals to dedicate themselves to their craft, continuously improving their skills, and striving for greatness in every endeavor.

DISCIPLINE AND CONSISTENCY:

Success demands discipline and consistency. Gates emphasizes the importance of staying focused, diligently working towards goals, and maintaining a consistent effort over time. This approach helps individuals build momentum and make progress even in the face of challenges.

Embracing Responsibility:

Gates' mantra underscores the significance of taking full responsibility for one's actions and outcomes. It encourages individuals to hold themselves accountable, rather than seeking external factors to blame for setbacks or failures.

Overcoming Obstacles:

"No Excuses" reflects Gates' belief that obstacles are not insurmountable barriers but opportunities for growth and learning. It encourages individuals to approach challenges with resilience, adaptability, and a determination to find solutions.

Maximizing Productivity:

Working hard involves maximizing productivity and making the most of available resources. Gates advocates for efficient time management, prioritization, and a focus on tasks that contribute most directly to one's goals.

Perseverance in the Face of Failure:

Gates recognizes that setbacks and failures are inevitable. However, his philosophy encourages individuals to view them as stepping stones towards success, embracing the lessons they offer, and using them as fuel for further growth.

Leading by Example:

As a prominent figure in the business world, Gates leads by example, showcasing the rewards of hard work and dedication. His unwavering commitment to his vision and tireless efforts have inspired countless individuals to push their limits and strive for greatness.

Bill Gates' "Work Hard, No Excuses" mantra serves as a reminder that success is not handed out but earned through perseverance, dedication, and an unwavering work ethic. By adopting this mindset, individuals can overcome challenges, seize opportunities, and unlock their full potential. Gates' enduring legacy stands as a testament to the transformative power of hard work, leaving a lasting inspiration for generations to come.

Bill Gates' "Work Hard, No Excuses" philosophy transcends the boundaries of success in the business world and extends into various aspects of life. It emphasizes the importance of taking ownership of one's actions, pushing beyond limits, and embracing the opportunities that come with hard work. Here, we delve further into the core principles underlying Gates' motto:

Continuous Improvement:

Gates believes in the value of constant growth and improvement. He encourages individuals to never settle for mediocrity but to continually strive for betterment in all areas of life. By seeking opportunities for learning and development, one can stay ahead of the curve and adapt to an ever-changing world.

Time Management and Prioritization:

To truly work hard and eliminate excuses, effective time management and prioritization are essential. Gates advocates for identifying the most crucial tasks and allocating time and resources accordingly. This ensures that efforts are directed towards activities that yield the greatest impact.

Resilience and Grit:

Achieving long-term success often requires resilience and the ability to bounce back from setbacks. Gates believes in cultivating a mindset of perseverance, refusing to let failures or obstacles deter progress. By embracing challenges and maintaining a strong resolve, individuals can forge ahead and achieve their goals.

Passion and Purpose:

Gates highlights the importance of aligning one's work with passion and purpose. When individuals are genuinely passionate about what they do, their motivation and drive are heightened, leading to increased productivity and satisfaction. It is the passion for their mission that fuels their determination to work hard and succeed.

Balancing Ambition and Well-being:

While "Work Hard, No Excuses" emphasizes dedication and commitment, Gates also recognizes the importance of maintaining a healthy work-life balance. He encourages individuals to prioritize their well-being and find harmony between their personal and professional lives. Taking care of physical and mental health enhances productivity and longevity in pursuing goals.

Embracing Feedback and Continuous Learning:

Gates firmly believes in the power of feedback and learning from others. He encourages individuals to seek constructive criticism, embrace diverse perspectives, and continuously refine their skills. By being open to feedback and actively seeking opportunities for growth, one can consistently improve and adapt to a rapidly changing world.

Impact and Making a Difference:

Beyond personal success, Gates emphasizes the importance of using one's influence and resources to make a positive impact on society. He believes that true fulfillment comes from leveraging success to address global challenges, promote equality, and improve the lives of others. By working hard and refusing to make excuses, individuals can contribute meaningfully to the world around them.

Bill Gates' "Work Hard, No Excuses" motto serves as a powerful reminder that success is not achieved through shortcuts or complacency but through unwavering dedication, perseverance, and a relentless pursuit of excellence. By embracing these principles, individuals can unlock their potential, exceed their own expectations, and leave a lasting impact on the world.

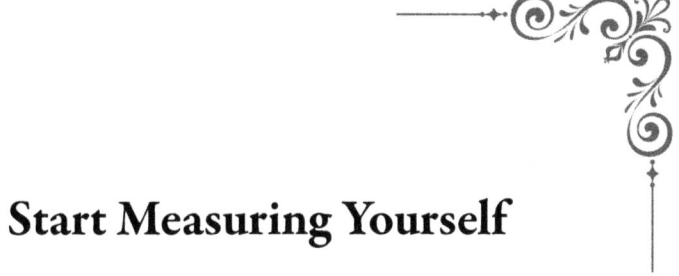

Start Measuring Yourself

Bill Gates' call to "Start Measuring Yourself" encapsulates his belief in the power of tracking progress, setting goals, and continuously evaluating one's growth. Recognizing that measurement is crucial for self-improvement and achieving success, Gates encourages individuals to adopt a mindset of self-assessment and accountability. In this section, we discover the significance of Gates' advice and its practical implications:

Setting Clear Goals:

To measure oneself effectively, setting clear and specific goals is paramount. Gates encourages individuals to define their objectives with precision, enabling them to track progress and determine the necessary steps for achievement. Well-defined goals provide a sense of direction and purpose.

Metrics for Progress:

Gates stresses the importance of identifying meaningful metrics to gauge progress. Whether it's financial targets, productivity indicators, or personal growth milestones, establishing measurable metrics enables individuals to assess their advancement objectively. Tracking these metrics helps in identifying areas that need improvement or adjustments.

Learning from Data:

Measurement involves analyzing data and drawing insights from it. Gates advocates for leveraging data to understand patterns, trends, and areas of strength or weakness. By extracting valuable insights, individuals can make informed decisions, refine strategies, and optimize their efforts.

Continuous Improvement:

Measuring oneself aligns with the pursuit of continuous improvement. Gates believes that regular evaluation of progress allows for ongoing refinement of skills, strategies, and processes. It enables individuals to iterate, learn from mistakes, and strive for incremental growth.

Course Correction:

Measuring oneself facilitates early detection of deviations from desired outcomes. Gates emphasizes the importance of promptly identifying areas where progress may be lacking or veering off track. By being aware of these deviations, individuals can make timely adjustments and course corrections to stay on the path towards their goals.

Accountability and Motivation:

Regular measurement fosters a sense of accountability. Gates encourages individuals to hold themselves responsible for their progress and take ownership of their actions. By tracking and measuring performance, individuals stay motivated, as progress becomes visible and milestones are achieved.

Celebrating Success:

Measurement not only highlights areas for improvement but also allows individuals to celebrate their successes. Gates advises individuals to acknowledge and appreciate milestones reached along the way. Celebrating achievements fuels motivation, boosts confidence, and provides encouragement to keep pushing forward.

Balancing Quantitative and Qualitative Measures:

While quantitative measures are often emphasized, Gates emphasizes the significance of qualitative assessment as well. It is essential to consider not only numerical data but also the qualitative aspects of personal growth and success. Evaluating values, ethics, and personal development ensures a holistic approach to measurement.

By embracing Gates' call to "Start Measuring Yourself," individuals can take charge of their progress, identify areas of improvement, and align their actions with their goals. Regular measurement, when combined with reflection and adjustments, fosters a growth-oriented mindset that propels individuals towards continuous improvement and achievement.

Don't Let Complexity Stop You

Bill Gates' statement, "Don't let complexity stop you," serves as a powerful reminder to embrace challenges and not be deterred by the complexities that often accompany ambitious goals. Gates recognizes that complex problems can be intimidating, but he encourages individuals to approach them with determination, resilience, and a commitment to finding solutions. Here, we discover the underlying principles and implications of Gates' advice:

Embracing Ambiguity:

Complexity often involves ambiguity and uncertainty. Gates encourages individuals to embrace the unknown and navigate through intricate situations with adaptability and an open mind. By embracing ambiguity, individuals can uncover innovative solutions and opportunities for growth.

Breaking Down Complexities:

Gates advocates for breaking down complex problems into manageable parts. Rather than being overwhelmed by the enormity of a challenge, individuals can tackle it systematically by identifying and addressing the underlying components. Breaking down complexities into smaller, more manageable tasks fosters progress and builds momentum.

Seeking Knowledge and Expertise:

To overcome complexity, Gates emphasizes the importance of seeking knowledge and expertise. He encourages individuals to tap into the collective wisdom of others, whether through collaboration, mentorship, or research. By leveraging the insights and experiences of experts, one can navigate through complex territories more effectively.

ITERATIVE PROBLEM-SOLVING:

Complex problems rarely have simple, straightforward solutions. Gates advocates for an iterative problem-solving approach, where individuals continuously learn, adapt, and refine their strategies based on feedback and insights gained along the way. This iterative process allows for experimentation, learning from mistakes, and ultimately reaching effective solutions.

Thinking Creatively:

Gates believes in the power of creative thinking to overcome complexity. By thinking outside the box, challenging conventional wisdom, and exploring alternative perspectives, individuals can uncover innovative approaches to complex problems. Creativity enables the discovery of breakthrough solutions that may not be apparent through traditional means.

COLLABORATION AND TEAMWORK:

Complex challenges often require collaborative efforts. Gates stresses the significance of teamwork and collaboration, bringing together individuals with diverse expertise and perspectives. By fostering an environment of collaboration, sharing knowledge, and leveraging collective strengths, complex problems become more manageable and solvable.

Perseverance and Resilience:

Complexity can test one's perseverance and resilience. Gates encourages individuals not to be deterred by setbacks or initial difficulties but to persist in the face of challenges. It is through persistence and resilience that breakthroughs are achieved and complex problems are conquered.

Learning from Complexity:

Rather than viewing complexity as a roadblock, Gates sees it as an opportunity for growth and learning. Complex problems provide valuable lessons and insights that can be applied to future endeavors. By embracing complexity, individuals can enhance their problem-solving skills, expand their knowledge base, and become more adept at handling challenges.

Gates' advice to "Don't let complexity stop you" serves as a reminder that complexity is not a barrier to success but an invitation to discover, innovate, and find solutions. By embracing challenges head-on, individuals can unlock their potential, overcome barriers, and make meaningful progress in their personal and professional endeavors.

Never Stop Learning

Bill Gates' resounding message of "Never Stop Learning" underscores the value he places on continuous education, personal growth, and intellectual curiosity. Gates recognizes that learning is not confined to formal education but extends throughout one's lifetime. By embracing a mindset of perpetual learning, individuals can adapt to new challenges, stay ahead of the curve, and continually expand their horizons. Here, we discover the profound significance and practical implications of Gates' advice:

Lifelong Intellectual Curiosity:

Gates encourages individuals to nurture a lifelong curiosity and thirst for knowledge. By embracing intellectual curiosity, individuals can remain open to new ideas, discover diverse subjects, and seek out learning opportunities that align with their interests.

Embracing New Technologies:

Gates acknowledges the transformative power of technology and its impact on various industries. He urges individuals to embrace new technologies, staying informed about their developments, and leveraging their potential for personal and professional growth.

Adapting to Change:

In a rapidly evolving world, adaptability is key. Gates emphasizes the importance of continuously adapting to change, whether it be technological advancements, shifts in the business landscape, or societal transformations. By embracing change, individuals can thrive in dynamic environments and seize new opportunities.

Expanding Knowledge and Skills:

Gates encourages individuals to expand their knowledge and skills beyond their areas of expertise. He advocates for a well-rounded approach to learning, exploring diverse subjects, and acquiring a broad range of skills that complement and enhance one's core competencies.

Learning from Diverse Sources:

Learning opportunities exist in various forms, including books, online resources, mentors, and personal experiences. Gates advises individuals to seek knowledge from diverse sources, drawing insights from different perspectives and disciplines. This multidimensional learning approach fosters a comprehensive understanding of complex issues.

Investing Time in Personal Growth:

Gates emphasizes the importance of allocating time for personal growth. Whether it involves attending seminars, pursuing online courses, or engaging in self-reflection, dedicating time to personal development allows individuals to continually enhance their skills, perspectives, and self-awareness.

Embracing Failure as a Learning Opportunity:

Gates sees failure not as an endpoint but as a valuable learning opportunity. He encourages individuals to reflect on their failures, analyze the reasons behind them, and extract lessons that can inform future endeavors. By embracing failure, individuals cultivate resilience, adaptability, and a growth mindset.

Cultivating a Culture of Learning:

Gates recognizes the value of fostering a culture of learning within organizations and communities. He encourages the creation of environments that support knowledge sharing, collaboration, and continuous improvement. By promoting a culture of learning, organizations and communities can drive innovation and adaptability.

Applying Knowledge to Make an Impact:

Gates believes that knowledge is most powerful when applied to make a positive impact on the world. He encourages individuals to use their learning and expertise to address pressing challenges, contribute to societal progress, and make a meaningful difference in the lives of others.

By embracing Bill Gates' mantra of "Never Stop Learning," individuals can cultivate a mindset of growth, adaptability, and intellectual curiosity. Through a commitment to continuous learning, individuals can navigate the complexities of the modern world, embrace new opportunities, and make significant contributions to their own lives and society as a whole.

Read Books

Bill Gates' straightforward advice to "Read Books" encapsulates his belief in the transformative power of reading. Gates is an avid reader himself and attributes much of his success to the knowledge and insights gained through books. By immersing oneself in the written word, individuals can expand their horizons, deepen their understanding, and unlock new possibilities. Here, we discover the profound impact and practical implications of Gates' emphasis on reading:

Acquiring Knowledge:

Books are a gateway to knowledge. Gates encourages individuals to read books across various genres and disciplines to broaden their understanding of the world. Whether it's non-fiction, fiction, or biographies, books provide valuable insights, ideas, and perspectives that can inform personal and professional growth.

Gaining Diverse Perspectives:

Reading exposes individuals to diverse perspectives and cultures. Gates advocates for exploring literature from different countries, time periods, and backgrounds to foster empathy, cultural understanding, and a broader worldview. It enables individuals to appreciate the complexities and richness of human experiences.

Nurturing Imagination and Creativity:

Books ignite the imagination and stimulate creativity. Gates believes that reading fictional works transports individuals to different worlds, sparks creativity, and expands imaginative thinking. It encourages individuals to discover new ideas and possibilities beyond the confines of their own experiences.

Developing Critical Thinking:

Reading cultivates critical thinking skills. Gates encourages individuals to engage with thought-provoking books that challenge their assumptions and stimulate intellectual discourse. By critically analyzing the ideas presented in books, individuals can develop their capacity for discernment, reasoned judgment, and logical reasoning.

Continuous Learning:

Books offer a continuous source of learning. Gates emphasizes that reading is a lifelong pursuit and encourages individuals to make reading a regular habit. By consistently engaging with books, individuals can stay intellectually stimulated, adapt to changing times, and continuously acquire new knowledge.

Personal Growth and Self-Reflection:

Reading facilitates personal growth and self-reflection. Gates advises individuals to choose books that inspire self-reflection, personal development, and introspection. By delving into books that discover themes of self-improvement, resilience, and self-discovery, individuals can gain insights into their own lives, goals, and values.

Improving Communication Skills:

Reading enhances communication skills. Gates recognizes that reading exposes individuals to various writing styles, vocabulary, and storytelling techniques. It expands one's vocabulary, improves articulation, and deepens the ability to express ideas effectively, both in writing and in verbal communication.

Building Empathy and Emotional Intelligence:

Books have the power to evoke empathy and build emotional intelligence. Gates suggests reading works of literature that delve into human emotions, relationships, and diverse experiences. By immersing oneself in these narratives, individuals can develop a greater understanding of others' perspectives, emotions, and struggles.

Finding Inspiration:

Books serve as a wellspring of inspiration. Gates highlights the transformative impact of reading stories of remarkable individuals, historical events, and societal transformations. These narratives inspire individuals to dream big, overcome challenges, and make a positive impact on the world.

By embracing Bill Gates' advice to "Read Books," individuals can unlock a treasure trove of knowledge, inspiration, and personal growth. Reading opens the door to new ideas, expands horizons, and cultivates a lifelong love of learning. It is through the pages of books that individuals can embark on intellectual adventures, gain wisdom from diverse voices, and embark on a transformative journey of self-discovery.

Do Volunteer Works

Bill Gates' encouragement to "Do Volunteer Works" reflects his commitment to making a positive impact on society and his belief in the power of individual actions to bring about change. Gates recognizes the transformative potential of volunteering, both for the communities being served and for the personal growth and fulfillment it brings. Here, we discover the profound significance and practical implications of Gates' emphasis on volunteer work:

Making a Difference:

Volunteer work enables individuals to directly contribute to causes they care about. Gates encourages individuals to actively engage in volunteer activities that align with their values and passions. By dedicating time and effort to meaningful projects, individuals can make a tangible difference in their communities and the lives of others.

Addressing Social Issues:

Volunteering provides an opportunity to address pressing social issues. Gates emphasizes the importance of actively participating in initiatives that tackle poverty, inequality, education, healthcare, environmental sustainability, and other critical challenges. Through volunteer work, individuals can contribute to building a more equitable and sustainable world.

Gaining Perspective and Empathy:

Volunteering exposes individuals to diverse experiences and perspectives. Gates believes that engaging with different communities and individuals fosters empathy, understanding, and compassion. It broadens one's perspective and cultivates a deeper appreciation for the struggles and aspirations of others.

Developing Skills and Building Networks:

Volunteer work offers a platform to develop new skills and expand professional networks. Gates suggests engaging in projects that provide opportunities for personal growth, whether it's leadership, teamwork, communication, or problem-solving. Volunteering also connects individuals with like-minded individuals and organizations, opening doors to future collaborations and opportunities.

Fostering Personal Growth:

Volunteer work nurtures personal growth and self-discovery. Gates recognizes that giving back to others can bring a sense of purpose, fulfillment, and personal satisfaction. Through volunteer experiences, individuals develop resilience, empathy, leadership skills, and a greater appreciation for their own blessings.

CREATING LASTING CHANGE:

Gates believes that volunteer work can be a catalyst for sustainable change. By actively participating in grassroots initiatives, advocacy campaigns, or community development projects, individuals can contribute to long-term solutions and empower communities to create positive change from within.

Inspiring Others:

Volunteerism serves as a powerful inspiration for others. Gates encourages individuals to lead by example and inspire others to get involved in volunteer work. By sharing personal experiences and the impact of their efforts, individuals can motivate and mobilize a broader movement towards collective action.

Philanthropic Leadership:

Gates sees volunteer work as an integral part of philanthropic leadership. He encourages individuals to combine their time, skills, and resources to address societal challenges effectively. Through volunteerism, individuals can complement their financial contributions with hands-on engagement, ensuring a more holistic and impactful approach to philanthropy.

Strengthening Communities:

Volunteer work strengthens the social fabric of communities. Gates believes that by actively engaging in volunteer activities, individuals contribute to creating a sense of belonging, social cohesion, and solidarity. Volunteerism fosters a shared responsibility for the well-being and progress of society.

By heeding Bill Gates' call to "Do Volunteer Works," individuals can actively contribute to positive change, empower others, and experience personal growth and fulfillment. Volunteering serves as a catalyst for creating a more compassionate, equitable, and resilient world. Through collective action, individuals can harness their skills, passion, and resources to make a lasting impact on society and leave a meaningful legacy.

Enjoy What You Do

Bill Gates' reminder to "Enjoy What You Do" underscores the importance of finding joy, passion, and fulfillment in one's work. Gates believes that true success lies not only in achieving goals but also in deriving personal satisfaction and happiness from the journey. Here, we discover the profound significance and practical implications of Gates' emphasis on enjoying what you do:

Fulfillment and Motivation:

Gates highlights that when individuals enjoy their work, they are more likely to be motivated, engaged, and committed to their tasks. Finding joy in what one does serves as an intrinsic source of motivation, driving individuals to give their best and persevere through challenges.

Aligning Passion and Purpose:

Gates encourages individuals to align their work with their passions and values. When there is a strong alignment between personal interests, skills, and the purpose of the work, individuals can experience a deep sense of fulfillment and meaning in their professional endeavors.

Sustained Commitment:

Enjoyment and satisfaction foster sustained commitment. Gates recognizes that individuals who find joy in their work are more likely to stay dedicated and committed for the long term. The enjoyment derived from the work becomes a driving force that helps individuals overcome obstacles and persevere through setbacks.

CREATIVITY AND INNOVATION:

Enjoying what you do fuels creativity and innovation. Gates believes that when individuals are passionate about their work, they are more likely to think creatively, discover new ideas, and find innovative solutions to challenges. Enjoyment provides the freedom to experiment, take risks, and push the boundaries of what is possible.

Work-Life Integration:

Gates acknowledges the importance of achieving a healthy work-life balance. By enjoying what you do, individuals can integrate work into their lives in a way that promotes well-being, personal relationships, and overall life satisfaction. When work is fulfilling and enjoyable, it complements other aspects of life, creating a sense of harmony.

Continuous Growth and Learning:

Enjoyment and curiosity go hand in hand. Gates emphasizes that when individuals enjoy their work, they are more likely to be curious, seek opportunities for learning, and continually grow in their professional skills and knowledge. The joy of learning becomes an inherent part of the work itself.

Positive Impact:

Gates believes that when individuals find joy in their work, they are more likely to make a positive impact on others and society. Enjoyment brings enthusiasm, empathy, and a genuine desire to contribute meaningfully. By bringing joy to their work, individuals can inspire and uplift others.

Role Modeling and Leadership:

Gates encourages individuals to lead by example and inspire others by finding joy in what they do. By demonstrating a positive and enthusiastic attitude towards their work, individuals can create a culture that promotes enjoyment, engagement, and overall well-being. Such leadership can inspire others to seek fulfillment in their own endeavors.

Personal Happiness and Well-being:

Ultimately, enjoying what you do contributes to personal happiness and well-being. Gates recognizes that individuals who find joy in their work experience a greater sense of fulfillment, satisfaction, and overall happiness in life. Enjoyment becomes a cornerstone of a fulfilling and meaningful existence.

By embracing Bill Gates' reminder to "Enjoy What You Do," individuals can cultivate a sense of joy, passion, and fulfillment in their professional pursuits. Through alignment with personal values, purpose, and a focus on the intrinsic rewards of work, individuals can create a pathway to success that nourishes their well-being, creativity, and overall life satisfaction.

Chapter 2: Elon Musk's 7 Rules of Investment

ELON MUSK, THE VISIONARY entrepreneur and business magnate known for his groundbreaking ventures such as Tesla, SpaceX, and Neuralink, has not only revolutionized industries but also established himself as one of the world's most influential figures in the realm of investment. With his bold and innovative approach to business, Musk has amassed significant wealth and achieved remarkable success in various ventures.

In addition to his achievements in technology and entrepreneurship, Musk has shared valuable insights into his investment strategies and principles. By distilling his experiences and observations, Musk has outlined seven key rules that can serve as a guide for those seeking financial success and prosperity. These principles, known as "The 7 Rules of Investment by Elon Musk," provide a framework for making informed investment decisions and navigating the complexities of the financial world.

In this book, we will delve into each of these rules, exploring the wisdom they offer and the impact they can have on one's investment journey. Whether you are a seasoned investor or just starting to discover the world of finance, Musk's rules provide valuable guidance and inspiration for achieving financial growth and building a successful investment portfolio.

Musk emphasizes the importance of having a long-term vision when it comes to investment. He advises investors to focus on long-term growth opportunities rather than short-term gains. Patience and the ability to weather market fluctuations are key to achieving substantial returns.

Musk encourages investors to seek out investments in disruptive technologies and industries that have the potential to transform the status quo. By identifying innovative and game-changing ventures, investors can position themselves for significant returns and growth.

Musk emphasizes the importance of thoroughly understanding the investment before committing capital. He advises investors to conduct in-depth research, analyze financial statements, and evaluate the company's fundamentals. A solid understanding of the investment is crucial for informed decision-making.

Musk advocates for risk management and diversification in investment portfolios. He advises investors to spread their investments across different asset classes, industries, and geographies to mitigate risk and protect against market volatility. Diversification helps balance potential losses and optimize returns.

Musk encourages investors to invest in companies and industries they truly believe in. By aligning investments with personal values and passions, investors can develop a deeper understanding of the businesses they support and make more informed decisions.

Musk emphasizes the importance of staying informed and continuously learning about the investment landscape. He advises investors to stay updated on industry trends, technological advancements, and market dynamics. A commitment to ongoing learning enables investors to adapt to changing market conditions and make strategic investment decisions.

Musk recognizes the need for calculated risk-taking in investment. He encourages investors to carefully assess risks and rewards, and to take calculated risks when the potential upside outweighs the downside. Taking strategic risks can lead to significant opportunities for growth and returns.

"The 7 Rules of Investment by Elon Musk" provide valuable insights into the mindset and strategies of one of the most successful entrepreneurs of our time. By applying these principles, investors can make informed decisions, seize opportunities, and navigate the intricacies of the financial world with confidence. Whether your investment journey is just beginning or you're seeking to refine your strategies, Musk's rules can serve as a guiding light on the path to financial success.

Focus on the Long Term

ELON MUSK, THE VISIONARY entrepreneur and business magnate behind transformative companies like Tesla, SpaceX, and Neuralink, has gained international acclaim for his innovative thinking and bold vision. One of the fundamental principles that underpins Musk's approach to business and investment is his unwavering focus on the long term. Musk understands that true success is not merely defined by short-term gains but by building sustainable ventures that have a lasting impact. In this book, we discover the significance and practical implications of Musk's emphasis on focusing on the long term.

Visionary Thinking:

Musk's focus on the long term is driven by his visionary mindset. He envisions a future shaped by groundbreaking technologies and industries that address pressing global challenges. By keeping his eyes fixed on the horizon, Musk maintains a sense of purpose and direction that guides his decisions and fuels his relentless pursuit of transformative ideas.

Building for the Future:

Musk's ventures, such as Tesla's electric vehicles and SpaceX's space book, exemplify his commitment to building for the future. He recognizes the need to address critical issues, like climate change and space book, with sustainable and long-term solutions. By focusing on the long term, Musk aims to create a positive impact that extends far beyond immediate financial gains.

Patience and Resilience:

A long-term focus requires patience and resilience. Musk understands that achieving ambitious goals often takes time and requires perseverance through challenges and setbacks. By maintaining a long-term perspective, he embraces the inevitable ups and downs of the entrepreneurial journey, remaining steadfast in his pursuit of game-changing advancements.

Innovation and Disruption:

Musk's long-term focus fuels his drive for innovation and disruption. Rather than conforming to existing norms, he continually pushes the boundaries of technology and industry standards. By challenging the status quo, Musk seeks to redefine possibilities and create lasting change in sectors that have traditionally resisted innovation.

Strategic Decision-Making:

A long-term perspective shapes Musk's decision-making process. He carefully evaluates the potential long-term impact and viability of each opportunity before committing resources. Musk's strategic decision-making prioritizes sustainable growth, innovation, and long-term value creation over short-term gains.

Sustainable Solutions:

Musk's focus on the long term extends to his commitment to sustainable solutions. He recognizes the urgency of addressing environmental and societal challenges, and his ventures reflect this commitment. By developing sustainable technologies, such as electric vehicles and renewable energy solutions, Musk aims to create a better future for generations to come.

Stakeholder Value Creation:

Musk's long-term focus extends beyond financial returns to encompass stakeholder value creation. He prioritizes the interests of customers, employees, and society as a whole, recognizing that long-term success is built on trust and positive relationships. By serving the needs of diverse stakeholders, Musk fosters loyalty, secures partnerships, and strengthens his ventures.

Legacy and Impact:

Musk's focus on the long term is rooted in his desire to leave a lasting legacy and make a significant impact on humanity. He envisions a future where sustainable energy, space book, and other transformative technologies shape society. By focusing on the long term, Musk seeks to leave a profound legacy that extends far beyond his own lifetime.

Elon Musk's emphasis on focusing on the long term serves as a guiding principle for those aspiring to create sustainable and impactful ventures. By maintaining a visionary mindset, making strategic decisions, and prioritizing innovation and stakeholder value creation, individuals and organizations can emulate Musk's commitment to building a better future. With a long-term perspective, they can navigate challenges, seize opportunities, and leave a lasting impact on the world.

Don't Follow the Crowd

ELON MUSK'S STRATEGY for success includes a key principle: "Don't Follow the Crowd." Musk has consistently demonstrated a willingness to challenge conventional thinking and take bold, unconventional approaches to achieve his goals. This mindset sets him apart as an innovator and disruptor in multiple industries. By not conforming to the norms and expectations set by others, Musk has achieved remarkable success. He encourages individuals to think independently, trust their instincts, and forge their own paths. Following the crowd can limit one's potential, while stepping outside the comfort zone and charting a unique course can lead to groundbreaking accomplishments. By embracing this philosophy, individuals can unleash their creativity, challenge established norms, and create lasting impact in their respective fields.

By refusing to follow the crowd, Elon Musk has shown a willingness to challenge traditional thinking and discover uncharted territories. This approach has been fundamental to his success in revolutionizing industries and pushing the boundaries of innovation. Here are further insights into the implications of Musk's strategy:

Embracing Risk and Uncertainty:

Musk's refusal to follow the crowd reflects his comfort with risk and uncertainty. He recognizes that groundbreaking achievements often involve venturing into the unknown and facing considerable risks. By embracing these challenges, Musk has been able to pioneer new technologies and industries, such as electric vehicles and private space book.

Thinking Outside the Box:

Musk encourages individuals to break free from conventional thinking and discover new possibilities. Rather than adhering to established norms, he seeks unconventional solutions to complex problems. This mindset has allowed him to challenge industry conventions and develop disruptive technologies that have reshaped entire sectors.

Trusting Intuition and Vision:

By not following the crowd, Musk emphasizes the importance of trusting one's intuition and vision. He believes that true innovators must have the courage to follow their instincts, even in the face of skepticism or opposition. Musk's audacious pursuits, such as his vision for a sustainable future and colonization of Mars, exemplify the power of unwavering belief in one's ideas.

Identifying Untapped Opportunities:

Musk's strategy involves seeking out untapped opportunities that others may overlook. Rather than competing in saturated markets, he identifies gaps and unmet needs, paving the way for disruptive breakthroughs. This ability to spot unique opportunities has enabled him to revolutionize industries traditionally considered resistant to change.

Persistence in the Face of Criticism:

Choosing not to follow the crowd often means facing criticism and skepticism. Musk's approach demonstrates the importance of persistence and resilience when met with opposition. He has weathered setbacks and persevered through challenges, remaining dedicated to his long-term vision even in the face of adversity.

Fostering Innovation and Change:

Musk's refusal to follow the crowd fosters a culture of innovation and change within his organizations. He encourages his teams to think independently, challenge assumptions, and discover new possibilities. This approach cultivates an environment that embraces risk-taking, encourages creativity, and attracts individuals who share a passion for pushing boundaries.

Carving a Unique Path:

By not following the crowd, Musk has forged a unique path that sets him apart as a visionary entrepreneur. His willingness to take calculated risks and diverge from the mainstream has allowed him to leave an indelible mark on industries such as automotive, aerospace, and renewable energy. Musk's accomplishments highlight the transformative power of embracing individuality and pursuing unconventional paths.

Elon Musk's strategy of not following the crowd is a testament to the importance of individuality, courage, and unconventional thinking in achieving remarkable success. By challenging the status quo, embracing risks, and trusting one's instincts, individuals can break new ground, drive innovation, and create lasting impact in their endeavors.

Understanding the Industry

Elon Musk's strategy for success includes a crucial element: "Understand the Industry." Musk emphasizes the significance of in-depth industry knowledge and understanding to make informed decisions and drive innovation. By immersing himself in the intricacies of various sectors, Musk has been able to identify opportunities, disrupt traditional models, and achieve remarkable success. Here are further insights into the implications of Musk's strategy:

Comprehensive Market Research:

Understanding the industry requires thorough market research. Musk believes in gathering extensive knowledge about the market dynamics, trends, and consumer demands. By conducting in-depth research, he can identify gaps and opportunities that others may overlook, positioning himself for strategic advantage.

Familiarity with Existing Technologies and Limitations:

To disrupt an industry, Musk emphasizes the importance of understanding existing technologies and their limitations. By gaining insights into current solutions, he can identify areas for improvement or develop innovative alternatives that challenge the status quo.

Identifying Pain Points and Unmet Needs:

Understanding the industry involves identifying pain points and unmet needs within a specific sector. Musk actively seeks to address these challenges by developing disruptive solutions that offer significant value to customers. By understanding the industry's pain points, he can drive meaningful change and capture market opportunities.

Immersion in Technical Details:

Musk believes in immersing himself in the technical intricacies of the industry. Whether it's electric vehicles, space book, or renewable energy, he invests time in understanding the underlying technologies, engineering principles, and scientific advancements. This deep technical understanding allows him to push the boundaries of what is possible and drive innovation.

Staying Abreast of Emerging Trends:

Remaining up to date with emerging trends and technologies is critical in understanding the industry. Musk actively monitors advancements, research, and breakthroughs, positioning himself at the forefront of innovation. By staying ahead of the curve, he can anticipate future trends and capitalize on emerging opportunities.

LEARNING FROM INDUSTRY Experts:

Musk values learning from industry experts to gain insights and perspectives. He engages with professionals and thought leaders in various fields, leveraging their expertise to enhance his understanding. This collaborative approach helps him develop a well-rounded understanding of the industry and uncover valuable insights.

Identifying Opportunities for Disruption:

By deeply understanding the industry, Musk can identify opportunities for disruption. He seeks to challenge established norms and revolutionize traditional approaches. This disruption-driven mindset allows him to introduce innovative solutions that reshape industries and create new markets.

Leveraging Synergies and Cross-Pollination:

Musk believes in leveraging synergies and cross-pollination across industries. By drawing inspiration from diverse sectors, he can introduce concepts and technologies from one industry into another, sparking innovative ideas and pushing the boundaries of innovation.

Focus on Innovation

Musk is renowned for his relentless pursuit of groundbreaking advancements and disruptive technologies that have reshaped industries. By prioritizing innovation, he has achieved remarkable success and revolutionized multiple sectors. Here are further insights into the implications of Musk's strategy:

Embracing a Forward-Thinking Mindset:

Musk advocates for a forward-thinking mindset that constantly seeks innovative solutions to complex problems. He believes in challenging the status quo and pushing the boundaries of what is possible. By embracing a mindset of continuous improvement and book, individuals can unlock new possibilities and drive meaningful change.

DISRUPTING TRADITIONAL Models:

Musk's strategy revolves around disrupting traditional industry models. He seeks to challenge established norms and introduce revolutionary concepts that redefine the way industries operate. By identifying opportunities for disruption, individuals can create new markets, redefine customer experiences, and gain a competitive edge.

Emphasizing Technological Advancements:

Technology plays a central role in Musk's focus on innovation. He harnesses the power of technological advancements to drive transformative change. By staying at the forefront of emerging technologies, individuals can identify opportunities to leverage advancements and develop innovative solutions that reshape industries.

Encouraging a Culture of Innovation:

Musk emphasizes the importance of fostering a culture of innovation within organizations. He believes in empowering individuals to think creatively, take risks, and challenge the status quo. By encouraging a culture that values and rewards innovation, individuals can unleash their full creative potential and drive meaningful progress.

Solving Real-World Problems:

Musk's approach to innovation revolves around solving real-world problems. He identifies pressing challenges, such as climate change and sustainable energy, and develops solutions that address these issues. By aligning innovation efforts with solving significant problems, individuals can create meaningful impact and contribute to a more sustainable future.

Iterative Improvement and Rapid Prototyping:

Musk advocates for an iterative improvement process and rapid prototyping. He believes in continuously refining and iterating on ideas, products, and processes to drive innovation. By embracing a mindset of continuous improvement, individuals can learn from failures, adapt quickly, and develop solutions that truly meet the needs of customers.

Bold Risk-Taking:

Musk's focus on innovation requires embracing bold risk-taking. He recognizes that significant breakthroughs often involve taking calculated risks and exploring uncharted territory. By embracing risk and learning from failures, individuals can gain valuable insights, refine their approaches, and propel innovation forward.

Collaboration and Partnerships:

Musk understands the value of collaboration and partnerships in driving innovation. He actively seeks collaboration with other visionaries, experts, and organizations to combine expertise, resources, and perspectives. By fostering collaborative relationships, individuals can leverage collective intelligence and accelerate the pace of innovation.

Elon Musk's strategy underscores the transformative power of disruptive thinking, technological advancements, and a relentless pursuit of solving real-world problems. By embracing innovation as a driving force, individuals can shape industries, create positive change, and leave a lasting impact.

Diversify Your Investment

Elon Musk's strategy for investment includes a key principle: "Diversify Your Investment." This concept emphasizes the importance of diversification and risk management in building a successful investment portfolio. By spreading investments across different asset classes and industries, individuals can mitigate risks and optimize returns. Here are further insights into the implications of Musk's strategy:

Diversification for Risk Mitigation:

Musk advocates for diversifying investment portfolios to reduce risk. By allocating investments across various asset classes, such as stocks, bonds, real estate, and commodities, individuals can minimize the impact of market fluctuations on their overall portfolio. Diversification helps balance risk and optimize returns over the long term.

Avoiding Overconcentration:

Musk cautions against over concentrating investments in a single company or industry. He recognizes the risks associated with relying too heavily on a particular investment, as unforeseen events can significantly impact its value. By spreading investments across different sectors, individuals can avoid overexposure to a single area and reduce vulnerability to industry-specific risks.

Balancing Risk and Reward:

Devastifying investments involves striking a balance between risk and reward. Musk advises individuals to assess the potential risks and rewards of each investment and adjust their portfolio accordingly. Balancing high-risk investments with more stable options can help individuals optimize returns while minimizing exposure to unnecessary risks.

ACTIVE MONITORING AND Adjustments:

Musk emphasizes the importance of actively monitoring investments and making adjustments as needed. Markets and industries evolve, and individual investments may perform differently over time. Regularly reviewing and rebalancing the portfolio allows individuals to adapt to changing market conditions and maintain the desired risk-return profile.

Long-Term Investment Perspective:

Devastifying investments aligns with Musk's long-term investment perspective. He recognizes that successful investing requires patience and a focus on long-term growth rather than short-term gains. By diversifying and devestifying investments, individuals can position themselves for sustained growth and weather short-term market volatility.

SEEKING PROFESSIONAL Advice:

Musk acknowledges the value of seeking professional advice when it comes to investment decisions. Consulting with financial advisors or investment professionals can provide individuals with valuable insights and expertise. These professionals can help individuals devise a personalized investment strategy that aligns with their financial goals and risk tolerance.

Embracing Financial Education:

Musk believes in the power of financial education. By continuously expanding one's knowledge of investment principles, strategies, and market dynamics, individuals can make informed decisions and take an active role in managing their investments. Educating oneself about the intricacies of investing can lead to more confident and successful decision-making.

Devestifying investments, as advocated by Elon Musk, enables individuals to manage risks, optimize returns, and build a resilient investment portfolio. By diversifying across asset classes and industries, individuals can reduce exposure to specific risks and position themselves for long-term growth. Musk's strategy underscores the importance of balancing risk and reward, monitoring investments, and seeking professional guidance. With a focus on devestification, individuals can navigate the complexities of investing and work towards achieving their financial goals.

Invest in What You Believe

ELON MUSK'S INVESTMENT strategy includes a key principle: "Invest in What You Believe In." Musk emphasizes the significance of aligning investments with one's personal values and passions. By investing in companies and industries that individuals genuinely believe in, they can develop a deeper understanding of the businesses they support and make more informed investment decisions. Here are further insights into the implications of Musk's strategy:

Alignment with Personal Values:

Musk encourages individuals to align their investments with their personal values. By investing in companies that promote social responsibility, sustainability, or other causes individuals care about, they can feel a sense of purpose and satisfaction in knowing that their investments align with their beliefs.

Developing a Deeper Understanding:

Investing in what one believes in requires a deeper understanding of the companies, industries, and markets involved. Musk suggests conducting thorough research and due diligence to gain insights into the businesses individuals choose to invest in. This understanding allows for informed decision-making and a more comprehensive view of investment opportunities.

Supporting Innovation and Disruption:

Investing in what one believes in often involves supporting innovative and disruptive companies or industries. Musk has been a trailblazer in this regard, investing in companies that challenge traditional models and pave the way for transformative advancements. By investing in innovative ventures, individuals can actively contribute to driving change and shaping the future.

Long-Term Perspective:

Musk's strategy of investing in what he believes in aligns with his long-term investment perspective. He emphasizes the importance of looking beyond short-term gains and focusing on sustainable growth and value creation. By investing in companies that align with one's beliefs and have long-term potential, individuals can position themselves for enduring success.

Impact Investing:

Investing in what one believes in can encompass impact investing, which seeks both financial returns and positive social or environmental impact. By allocating capital to companies or projects that address critical societal or environmental challenges, individuals can contribute to making a difference while generating financial returns.

Active Engagement:

Investing in what one believes in often leads to active engagement and support for the companies or causes invested in. Musk advocates for staying informed, attending shareholder meetings, and actively participating in governance processes. By engaging with invested companies, individuals can have a voice in influencing their direction and impact.

Personal Satisfaction and Fulfillment:

Investing in what one believes in brings a sense of personal satisfaction and fulfillment. By supporting companies and industries that align with their passions, individuals can feel a stronger connection to their investments and derive a sense of purpose beyond financial returns. This alignment can enhance overall investment experience and personal well-being.

Elon Musk's strategy of investing in what one believes in underscores the importance of aligning investments with personal values, fostering a deeper understanding, and actively contributing to meaningful change. By investing in companies and industries individuals are passionate about, they can have a more profound impact, experience personal satisfaction, and work towards creating a future that aligns with their values and aspirations.

Stay Focused and Committed

Staying focused and committed is a crucial aspect of Elon Musk's approach to success. Musk recognizes that maintaining unwavering focus and dedication is essential for overcoming challenges, achieving long-term goals, and making significant strides in various endeavors. Here are further insights into the implications of Musk's emphasis on staying focused and committed:

Clear Goal Orientation:

Musk emphasizes the importance of setting clear goals and staying focused on them. By defining specific objectives, individuals can direct their efforts and resources towards achieving those targets. This clarity of purpose helps individuals maintain focus amidst distractions and prioritize tasks that align with their goals.

Perseverance in the Face of Challenges:

Staying focused and committed involves persevering through challenges and setbacks. Musk acknowledges that the path to success is often accompanied by obstacles and failures. However, he encourages individuals not to be discouraged by setbacks but to view them as opportunities for growth and learning. Maintaining unwavering commitment helps individuals navigate difficulties and persevere in their pursuit of success.

Discipline and Time Management:

Musk emphasizes the importance of discipline and effective time management. Staying focused requires individuals to allocate their time and energy to tasks that contribute to their goals. By prioritizing important activities and minimizing distractions, individuals can maximize productivity and progress towards their desired outcomes.

LONG-TERM VISION:

Commitment and focus go hand in hand with having a long-term vision. Musk advocates for thinking beyond immediate results and keeping the bigger picture in mind. By maintaining a long-term perspective, individuals can sustain motivation, make decisions that align with their ultimate objectives, and overcome short-term challenges.

Continuous Learning and Adaptation:

Staying focused and committed involves a commitment to continuous learning and adaptation. Musk emphasizes the importance of staying updated on industry trends, technological advancements, and market dynamics. By proactively seeking knowledge and adapting to changing circumstances, individuals can refine their strategies, make informed decisions, and remain at the forefront of innovation.

AVOIDING DISTRACTIONS:

Musk encourages individuals to minimize distractions that can derail focus and commitment. In an increasingly connected world, distractions abound, and staying focused requires deliberate effort. By prioritizing tasks, setting boundaries, and eliminating unnecessary distractions, individuals can maintain the clarity and concentration needed to achieve their goals.

Surrounding Oneself with Supportive Networks:

Musk recognizes the value of surrounding oneself with supportive networks. Building a team of like-minded individuals who share a common vision can enhance focus and commitment. Collaborating with individuals who share similar goals and values fosters a sense of collective commitment, accountability, and mutual support.

ALIGNMENT OF PASSION and Purpose:

Staying focused and committed is easier when individuals align their passion with their purpose. Musk encourages individuals to pursue endeavors that genuinely inspire them and align with their values. When individuals are passionate about their work, they are more likely to stay committed, overcome challenges, and achieve long-term success.

By staying focused and committed, individuals can navigate challenges, maintain momentum, and make meaningful progress towards their goals. Elon Musk's emphasis on these qualities highlights their transformative power in driving success and achieving remarkable outcomes.

Chapter 3: Warren Buffett's 6 Investment Principles

WARREN BUFFETT, WIDELY regarded as one of the greatest investors of all time, has built his legendary reputation on a set of six fundamental investment principles. These guiding principles have not only fueled Buffett's own success but have also served as a beacon of wisdom for countless investors around the world. Through decades of experience and a consistent focus on value investing, Buffett has amassed an incredible fortune and become a respected voice in the world of finance.

In this book, we delve into Warren Buffett's six investment principles, unveiling the timeless strategies that have shaped his remarkable career and can guide investors on their path to financial prosperity. These principles, honed over years of astute decision-making and disciplined investing, offer valuable insights into Buffett's approach and highlight key considerations for investors seeking to emulate his success.

Buffett's investment philosophy centers on value investing, which involves seeking undervalued companies with strong fundamentals. By focusing on intrinsic value and buying stocks at a discount, Buffett aims to capitalize on long-term growth potential and generate superior returns.

Buffett advocates for a patient and long-term approach to investing. He believes that successful investors should be willing to hold onto quality investments for extended periods, allowing them to benefit from compounding returns and avoid short-term market fluctuations.

Margin of Safety: Buffett emphasizes the importance of a margin of safety when evaluating potential investments. By purchasing assets at prices significantly below their intrinsic value, investors can protect themselves against unexpected market downturns or unforeseen risks.

Buffett's investment principles prioritize investing in high-quality companies with sustainable competitive advantages or "economic moats." Such businesses have a higher likelihood of enduring success, generating consistent cash flows, and providing solid returns over time.

Buffett stresses the significance of thoroughly understanding the businesses in which one invests. By conducting comprehensive research and analysis, investors can gain insights into the company's operations, competitive positioning, and industry dynamics, enabling informed decision-making.

Buffett encourages investors to exercise patience and maintain emotional discipline in the face of market volatility. He advises against succumbing to impulsive buying or selling decisions driven by short-term market fluctuations. Maintaining a long-term perspective and avoiding emotional reactions are essential for successful investing.

By embracing Warren Buffett's six investment principles, investors can gain valuable insights into his time-tested strategies and apply them to their own investment approach. These principles emphasize the importance of value, patience, disciplined research, and a long-term perspective. With a focus on these fundamental principles, investors can navigate the complexities of the financial markets and work towards achieving their own financial goals.

Cash is Not a Good Investment

Warren Buffett famously stated, "Cash is not a good investment." This succinct statement encapsulates Buffett's view on the limited potential of holding cash as a long-term investment strategy. Buffett believes that cash, while providing liquidity and stability, does not generate significant returns over time. Here are further insights into the implications of Buffett's stance:

Opportunity Cost: Buffett's perspective on cash as a poor investment reflects the concept of opportunity cost. By holding cash, investors forgo potential returns that could be generated by deploying those funds into other productive assets such as stocks, bonds, or real estate. The opportunity cost of holding cash becomes more apparent over the long term.

Inflation Erosion: Holding cash exposes investors to the risk of inflation erosion. Over time, the purchasing power of cash diminishes due to rising prices and the eroding effects of inflation. By allocating funds to investments that outpace inflation, investors can preserve and grow their wealth more effectively.

Potential for Capital Appreciation: Buffett emphasizes the importance of investing in assets that have the potential for capital appreciation. Unlike cash, which provides limited growth, investments in productive assets offer the possibility of generating returns through dividend income, interest payments, and capital gains.

Long-Term Value Creation: Buffett's aversion to cash as an investment reflects his focus on long-term value creation. He believes in investing in businesses and assets that have the potential to generate sustainable returns and increase in value over time. By investing in productive assets, individuals can participate in the wealth creation potential of businesses and the economy.

Risk Mitigation through Diversification: Buffett advocates for diversifying investments across a range of asset classes and industries. By spreading investments beyond cash, individuals can mitigate risk and capture potential returns from different sectors of the economy. Diversification helps protect against the risk of holding a single asset, such as cash, that may not perform well under certain market conditions.

Time Value of Money: Buffett's perspective on cash aligns with the concept of the time value of money. He recognizes that the value of money today is greater than the value of the same amount in the future due to the potential for investments to grow over time. By deploying cash into investments, individuals can harness the power of compounding and achieve higher returns over the long term.

Warren Buffett's statement, "Cash is not a good investment," underscores the importance of considering alternative investment options that have the potential to generate higher returns and preserve purchasing power over time. While cash provides stability and liquidity, it lacks the growth potential offered by productive assets. By allocating funds to investments that align with one's financial goals and risk tolerance, individuals can pursue long-term wealth accumulation and financial success.

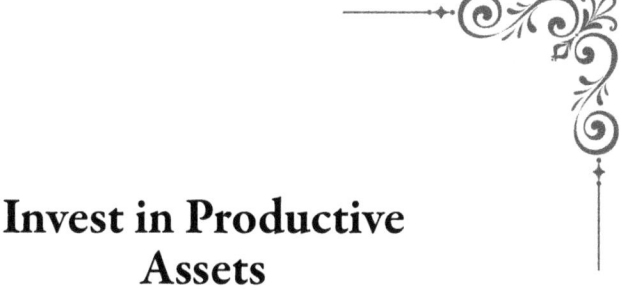

Invest in Productive Assets

Warren Buffett advocates for investing in productive assets as a key strategy for long-term financial success. Buffett believes that productive assets, such as businesses and real estate, have the potential to generate sustainable returns and increase in value over time. Here are further insights into the implications of Buffett's emphasis on investing in productive assets:

Ownership of Profitable Businesses: Buffett encourages investors to consider owning shares in profitable businesses. By investing in well-managed companies with strong competitive advantages, individuals can benefit from the company's earnings and potential capital appreciation. Owning shares in productive businesses allows individuals to participate in the wealth creation potential of those companies.

Focus on Quality and Long-Term Value: Buffett emphasizes the importance of investing in high-quality assets that have the potential for long-term value creation. He looks for companies with durable competitive advantages, solid management teams, and strong financial fundamentals. By focusing on quality, individuals can increase their chances of realizing sustainable returns from their investments.

Real Estate Investments: Buffett also recognizes the value of investing in real estate as a productive asset. Real estate can provide a stable income stream through rental properties and the potential for appreciation over time. By carefully evaluating properties and considering factors such as location and market trends, individuals can make informed real estate investments.

Dividend-Yielding Stocks: Buffett places importance on investing in dividend-yielding stocks. Dividends are a portion of a company's profits distributed to shareholders, providing investors with a regular income stream. By selecting stocks of companies with a history of consistent dividend payments and a strong financial position, individuals can benefit from both dividend income and potential stock price appreciation.

Long-Term Focus: Buffett's strategy of investing in productive assets aligns with his long-term perspective. He advises investors to take a patient approach, focusing on the long-term value and potential growth of their investments. By avoiding short-term market fluctuations and staying committed to their investment strategies, individuals can potentially benefit from the compounding effect of returns over time.

Potential for Cash Flow and Wealth Accumulation: Productive assets have the potential to generate cash flow and contribute to long-term wealth accumulation. Whether through business profits, rental income, or dividend payments, investing in productive assets provides individuals with opportunities to generate ongoing returns and build wealth over time.

Active Management and Due Diligence: Buffett emphasizes the importance of active management and thorough due diligence when investing in productive assets. It involves carefully analyzing financial statements, understanding industry dynamics, and staying informed about the companies or properties in which one invests. This active approach enables individuals to make informed investment decisions and actively monitor the performance of their investments.

By investing in productive assets, individuals can potentially benefit from the growth and income generation capabilities of businesses and real estate. Warren Buffett's strategy of focusing on quality, long-term value, and active management underscores the importance of carefully selecting and nurturing investments that have the potential for sustainable returns. Through a disciplined approach and a focus on productive assets, individuals can work towards achieving their financial goals and building long-term wealth.

Stay in Your Circle of Competence

Buffett emphasizes the importance of investing in businesses and industries that one understands well. By staying within their areas of expertise, investors can make informed decisions and avoid unnecessary risks. Here are further insights into the implications of Buffett's principle:

Know What You Know: Buffett encourages investors to assess their own knowledge, skills, and experience. By understanding their strengths and limitations, individuals can focus their investments on areas where they have a deep understanding. This knowledge-based approach allows for more informed decision-making and reduces the likelihood of making uninformed investment choices.

Stick to Familiar Industries: Buffett advises investors to stick to industries they are familiar with and understand deeply. Investing in industries one knows well enables individuals to better evaluate business models, assess competitive advantages, and identify potential risks. This familiarity enhances the ability to identify quality companies and make prudent investment decisions.

Avoid Speculation and Complex Investments: Buffett cautions against engaging in speculative investments or complex financial instruments outside of one's circle of competence. Investing in assets that are overly complex or difficult to understand increases the risk of making poor decisions based on incomplete information. By focusing on what one knows, individuals can avoid unnecessary complications and reduce the chances of significant losses.

Conduct Thorough Research: Staying within one's circle of competence requires conducting thorough research and analysis. Buffett emphasizes the importance of evaluating a company's financials, industry dynamics, competitive positioning, and future prospects. This research-intensive approach helps individuals make well-informed investment choices based on a deep understanding of the underlying businesses.

Patience and Discipline: Buffett's principle of staying in one's circle of competence aligns with the virtues of patience and discipline. It involves resisting the temptation to invest in areas outside of one's expertise, even when others may appear to be achieving significant returns. By adhering to a disciplined approach and maintaining patience, individuals can avoid hasty decisions and focus on opportunities that align with their circle of competence.

Continuous Learning and Expansion: Buffett encourages individuals to expand their circle of competence through continuous learning. While staying within one's existing knowledge base is crucial, it is also important to actively seek new opportunities for growth and learning. By expanding knowledge and expertise, individuals can gradually broaden their circle of competence and discover new investment possibilities.

Risk Mitigation: Staying within one's circle of competence helps mitigate risks associated with investing in unfamiliar areas. By focusing on industries and companies that one understands well, individuals can more accurately assess potential risks and make informed judgments about the prospects and challenges faced by the investments they consider.

Adhering to Warren Buffett's principle of staying within their circle of competence, investors can make more informed investment decisions and reduce unnecessary risks. By leveraging their expertise and conducting thorough research, individuals can increase their chances of achieving successful outcomes. This focused approach promotes prudent investing and aligns investments with one's knowledge and understanding, ultimately leading to more informed and potentially profitable investment choices.

Evaluate Companies First

"Evaluate Companies First" is a key principle advocated by Warren Buffett. Buffett emphasizes the importance of thoroughly evaluating companies before making investment decisions. By conducting a comprehensive analysis of a company's financial health, competitive positioning, management team, and growth prospects, investors can make informed choices and identify high-quality investment opportunities. Here are further insights into the implications of Buffett's principle:

Financial Analysis: Buffett advises investors to analyze a company's financial statements, including its balance sheet, income statement, and cash flow statement. By assessing key financial metrics, such as revenue growth, profitability, debt levels, and cash flow generation, individuals can evaluate the company's financial health and stability.

Competitive Advantage: Buffett places significant emphasis on identifying companies with a sustainable competitive advantage. A strong competitive position enables a company to outperform its competitors and generate consistent profits over time. By evaluating a company's moat, which could be based on factors such as branding, intellectual property, or cost leadership, investors can assess the likelihood of long-term success.

Management Team: Buffett believes in evaluating the competence and integrity of a company's management team. Strong leadership is crucial to driving business success and executing strategic initiatives. Assessing the track record, experience, and alignment of interests with shareholders helps investors gauge the quality of the management team.

Growth Prospects: Evaluating a company's growth prospects is a key consideration for investors. Buffett looks for companies with sustainable growth potential and a clear plan for future expansion. Analyzing industry trends, market opportunities, and the company's ability to innovate provides insights into its potential for long-term growth.

Valuation: Buffett emphasizes the importance of assessing a company's valuation relative to its intrinsic value. By estimating the intrinsic value of a business, investors can determine whether the current market price offers an attractive opportunity. Evaluating valuation ratios, such as price-to-earnings (P/E) or price-to-book (P/B), helps in determining whether a company is trading at a discount or premium.

Risk Assessment: Buffett encourages investors to evaluate the risks associated with an investment. This includes analyzing industry-specific risks, company-specific risks, and external factors that may impact the company's operations and financial performance. Understanding and assessing risks help investors make more informed decisions and develop risk management strategies.

Long-Term Perspective: Buffett's principle of evaluating companies first aligns with his long-term investment perspective. He believes in investing in companies with durable competitive advantages and solid growth prospects. By focusing on the long-term potential of a company rather than short-term market fluctuations, individuals can make investment decisions with a view to long-term value creation.

By following Buffett's principle of evaluating companies first, investors can make informed decisions based on a thorough assessment of the company's financial health, competitive advantages, management quality, growth prospects, and valuation. This approach promotes a more comprehensive understanding of investment opportunities, aligning investment decisions with the potential for long-term success and wealth creation.

Play Big and Don't Waste Opportunity

"Play Big and Don't Waste Opportunity" reflects Warren Buffett's philosophy towards maximizing success and capitalizing on opportunities. Buffett encourages individuals to embrace ambitious goals and seize opportunities that come their way. Here are further insights into the implications of Buffett's principle:

Embrace Ambition: Buffett's principle emphasizes the importance of setting ambitious goals. He encourages individuals to think big and not limit their aspirations. By setting high expectations and pushing beyond comfort zones, individuals can unlock their full potential and achieve remarkable success.

Take Calculated Risks: Buffett believes in taking calculated risks when opportunities arise. He encourages individuals to carefully evaluate the potential rewards and risks associated with an opportunity. While avoiding reckless decisions, calculated risks can lead to significant growth and reward.

Seize Opportunities: Buffett emphasizes the significance of seizing opportunities when they present themselves. Opportunities are not infinite, and individuals should be proactive in identifying and capitalizing on them. Buffett's success is attributed, in part, to his ability to recognize and act upon favorable opportunities in the market.

Avoid Wasting Time: Buffett cautions against wasting time on unproductive activities or pursuits that do not align with one's goals.

He advocates for prioritizing tasks that contribute to personal and professional growth and avoiding distractions that hinder progress. By utilizing time effectively, individuals can make the most of their opportunities and optimize their chances of success.

Learn from Mistakes: Buffett acknowledges that mistakes are inevitable, but he urges individuals not to waste the lessons they provide. Learning from mistakes is crucial in personal and professional development. By analyzing failures and making adjustments, individuals can grow wiser and improve their decision-making skills, increasing their chances of success in future endeavors.

Persevere Through Challenges: Buffett's principle of playing big and not wasting opportunity underscores the importance of perseverance in the face of challenges. He recognizes that setbacks and obstacles are part of the journey towards success. By maintaining determination and resilience, individuals can navigate challenges, learn from setbacks, and keep moving forward.

Long-Term Focus: Buffett's philosophy of playing big aligns with his long-term perspective. He advises individuals to focus on sustained success rather than short-term gains. By making strategic decisions that align with long-term goals, individuals can build a solid foundation for lasting achievements and avoid being swayed by short-lived trends.

Invest in Yourself

Warren Buffett emphasizes the importance of investing in oneself. Buffett believes that the best investment an individual can make is in their own personal development and acquiring knowledge. Here are further insights into the implications of Buffett's principle:

Continuous Learning: Buffett encourages individuals to engage in lifelong learning. He advocates for the pursuit of knowledge across various domains, including business, finance, and personal growth. By consistently expanding one's knowledge and staying intellectually curious, individuals can enhance their decision-making abilities and adapt to changing circumstances.

Personal Development: Buffett believes in investing time and effort in personal development. This involves honing skills, cultivating positive habits, and fostering a growth mindset. By continuously improving oneself, individuals can enhance their capabilities and increase their value in various aspects of life.

Acquire Expertise: Buffett advises individuals to acquire expertise in areas of interest or professional relevance. By becoming an expert in a particular field, individuals can differentiate themselves, seize unique opportunities, and command a higher value in the marketplace. Acquiring specialized knowledge enhances one's ability to make informed decisions and uncover potential investment opportunities.

Expand Your Network: Buffett recognizes the value of building a strong network of relationships. By connecting with like-minded individuals, industry experts, and mentors, individuals can gain valuable insights, access new opportunities, and receive guidance. Building a network of trusted advisors and collaborators contributes to personal growth and expands one's sphere of influence.

Emotional Intelligence: Buffett stresses the significance of developing emotional intelligence. Understanding and managing one's emotions, as well as effectively navigating interpersonal relationships, are crucial skills for success. Emotional intelligence fosters effective communication, collaboration, and decision-making, enabling individuals to navigate challenges and build strong professional and personal connections.

Prioritize Well-Being: Buffett's principle of investing in oneself extends to prioritizing personal well-being. He recognizes that physical and mental well-being are essential for sustained success. By adopting healthy habits, maintaining work-life balance, and managing stress, individuals can optimize their performance and make better investment decisions.

Take Calculated Risks: Buffett encourages individuals to take calculated risks in pursuing personal and professional growth. This may involve stepping outside one's comfort zone, embracing new challenges, and being open to learning from both successes and failures. Taking calculated risks fosters personal growth, expands capabilities, and opens doors to new opportunities.

By investing in oneself, individuals can enhance their knowledge, skills, and personal attributes, positioning themselves for greater success in various endeavors, including investing. Buffett's principle underscores the importance of continuous learning, personal development, and prioritizing well-being. By making ongoing investments in oneself, individuals can unlock their full potential, increase their value, and achieve meaningful outcomes in both personal and financial aspects of life.

Chapter 4: Robert Kiyosaki's 6 Basic Rules for Investment

ROBERT KIYOSAKI, ACCLAIMED author and investor, has established a set of six basic rules for investment that provide valuable insights and guidance to individuals seeking financial success. Kiyosaki's principles offer a framework for making informed investment decisions and building wealth over the long term. In this book, we delve into Kiyosaki's six basic rules for investment, exploring the core principles that underpin his approach and examining how they can shape the investment strategies of individuals looking to secure their financial future. By understanding and applying these rules, investors can gain a solid foundation for navigating the complex world of investing and working towards their financial goals.

Kiyosaki's six basic rules for investment serve as a roadmap for individuals seeking to make sound financial decisions and create a sustainable investment portfolio. These rules offer insights into Kiyosaki's investment philosophy and highlight key considerations for investors of all levels of experience. By embracing these principles, individuals can gain a better understanding of how to approach investing and work towards achieving their financial aspirations. In the following sections, we will discover each of these rules in detail, unveiling the wisdom behind Kiyosaki's approach and how they can be applied to build a solid foundation for investment success.

Kiyosaki emphasizes the importance of generating positive cash flow from investments. He advocates for investing in assets that produce regular income, such as rental properties, dividend-paying stocks, or profitable businesses. By focusing on cash flow, investors can ensure a consistent stream of income to cover expenses and reinvest for further growth.

Kiyosaki advises investors to diversify their portfolios across different asset classes and industries. This spreads risk and minimizes the impact of potential losses. By allocating investments across a range of assets, individuals can benefit from different market cycles and reduce their vulnerability to a single investment's performance.

Kiyosaki places great emphasis on continuous education. He believes that investing in one's financial intelligence is crucial for making informed decisions. By seeking out educational resources, attending seminars, and learning from experienced investors, individuals can enhance their understanding of investment strategies and develop the skills necessary for successful investing.

Kiyosaki encourages investors to adopt a long-term perspective. He advises against chasing short-term gains and instead focuses on building a solid investment foundation for the future. By taking a patient approach and focusing on long-term growth potential, individuals can potentially benefit from the power of compounding and weather short-term market fluctuations.

Kiyosaki stresses the importance of managing risks in investment. He advises individuals to conduct thorough due diligence, assess potential risks, and implement risk management strategies. By understanding the risks associated with an investment and taking steps to mitigate them, individuals can protect their capital and preserve wealth.

Kiyosaki reminds investors to maintain emotional control and avoid making impulsive investment decisions driven by fear or greed. He believes that emotions can cloud judgment and lead to irrational decision-making. By keeping emotions in check and making logical, well-informed choices, individuals can navigate investment markets with a greater sense of control.

By following Robert Kiyosaki's six basic rules for investment, individuals can gain a solid foundation for building their investment portfolios and working towards financial independence. These rules emphasize the importance of cash flow, diversification, education, long-term thinking, risk management, and emotional control. Applying these principles to investment strategies can help individuals make informed decisions, minimize risks, and increase the likelihood of achieving their financial goals.

Borrowing to Invest

Robert Kiyosaki has discoverd the concept of "Borrowing to Invest" as a strategy to potentially accelerate wealth creation. Kiyosaki challenges conventional thinking that debt is always detrimental and encourages individuals to leverage borrowed funds to invest in income-generating assets. Here are further insights into the implications of Kiyosaki's viewpoint:

Leveraging Other People's Money: Kiyosaki advocates for using other people's money, such as loans or credit, to invest in income-producing assets. The idea is to generate returns that surpass the cost of borrowing, thereby increasing wealth at an accelerated rate. By strategically using borrowed funds, individuals can access larger investment opportunities and potentially amplify their returns.

Focus on Positive Cash Flow: Kiyosaki stresses the importance of investing in assets that generate positive cash flow. This means that the income generated from the investment exceeds the cost of borrowing, allowing individuals to cover their debt obligations and generate additional income. Positive cash flow provides a buffer against potential financial challenges and supports the sustainability of the investment strategy.

Risk Management and Due Diligence: Kiyosaki highlights the need for thorough risk management and due diligence when borrowing to invest. It is crucial to carefully assess the investment opportunity, understand the potential risks involved, and ensure that the projected returns justify the cost of borrowing. Sound financial analysis and a well-informed investment decision are essential for minimizing potential risks.

Time Horizon and Market Conditions: Kiyosaki emphasizes the importance of considering the time horizon and market conditions when borrowing to invest. Longer time horizons provide more opportunities for investments to generate returns that exceed borrowing costs. Additionally, favorable market conditions, such as low interest rates or undervalued assets, can increase the potential for successful outcomes.

Financial Discipline: Kiyosaki advises individuals to maintain financial discipline when implementing a borrowing-to-invest strategy. This includes managing cash flows effectively, staying committed to debt repayment obligations, and having contingency plans in place. Financial discipline ensures that individuals can navigate potential challenges and take advantage of opportunities that arise.

Educating Oneself: Kiyosaki underscores the importance of financial education when considering borrowing to invest. Understanding the dynamics of borrowing, interest rates, investment analysis, and risk management is crucial for making informed decisions. By continuously expanding one's financial knowledge, individuals can enhance their ability to leverage borrowed funds effectively.

It is important to note that borrowing to invest carries inherent risks, including the potential for higher debt obligations and the volatility of investment returns. Individuals considering this strategy should carefully assess their risk tolerance, financial situation, and consult with financial professionals to determine if it aligns with their goals and circumstances.

Robert Kiyosaki's viewpoint on borrowing to invest challenges traditional notions of debt and presents an alternative approach to wealth creation. By utilizing borrowed funds strategically, investing in income-generating assets, and practicing sound risk management, individuals may have the potential to accelerate their wealth-building journey.

Passive Income

Robert Kiyosaki emphasizes the significance of generating passive income as a means of achieving financial independence and creating lasting wealth. Kiyosaki defines passive income as income generated from assets that work for you, allowing individuals to earn money even when they are not actively involved in the day-to-day operations. Here are further insights into the implications of Kiyosaki's emphasis on passive income:

Diversify Income Streams: Kiyosaki encourages individuals to diversify their income streams and reduce reliance on a single source of income, such as a job or salary. By building multiple streams of passive income from various assets, such as rental properties, dividend-paying stocks, or royalties from intellectual property, individuals can create a more resilient financial foundation.

Creating Financial Freedom: Passive income provides individuals with the opportunity to achieve financial freedom. It offers the possibility of earning more than their living expenses, thereby providing flexibility and the ability to pursue personal goals and passions. By generating sufficient passive income, individuals can break free from the constraints of relying solely on active income.

Building Wealth Over Time: Kiyosaki highlights that passive income has the potential to build wealth over time. As individuals accumulate and reinvest their passive income, their asset base grows, leading to compounding returns and an increasing stream of passive income. This wealth-building process can provide financial stability and a path to long-term prosperity.

Time and Location Freedom: Passive income enables individuals to have more control over their time and location. With passive income streams in place, individuals can have the freedom to choose how they spend their time and where they live. This flexibility allows for a better work-life balance and the opportunity to prioritize experiences and relationships.

Scalability and Leverage: Passive income often offers scalability and the potential for leverage. Certain assets, such as real estate or online businesses, can be scaled up to generate larger streams of passive income. Additionally, individuals can leverage their resources, such as borrowing to acquire income-generating assets, to increase their passive income potential.

Focus on Asset Accumulation: Kiyosaki emphasizes the importance of accumulating income-generating assets to generate passive income. He encourages individuals to prioritize acquiring assets that produce cash flow over liabilities that drain financial resources. By focusing on building a portfolio of income-generating assets, individuals can increase their passive income potential over time.

Continuous Learning and Adaptation: Kiyosaki highlights the need for continuous learning and adaptation to generate and grow passive income. Staying informed about investment opportunities, market trends, and evolving technologies enables individuals to identify new income streams and adapt their strategies accordingly. Being proactive and open to learning enhances the ability to generate sustainable passive income.

Passive income provides the opportunity for financial freedom, wealth accumulation, and a more flexible lifestyle. By building a portfolio of income-generating assets and continually expanding financial knowledge, individuals can work towards achieving financial independence and creating a more secure financial future.

Financial Education

Robert Kiyosaki places a strong emphasis on the importance of financial education as a key pillar for achieving financial success and independence. Kiyosaki believes that a solid foundation of financial knowledge is essential for making informed decisions, navigating the complexities of the financial world, and building lasting wealth. Here are further insights into the implications of Kiyosaki's emphasis on financial education:

Understanding Money and Investing: Kiyosaki encourages individuals to educate themselves about the fundamentals of money and investing. This includes understanding concepts such as cash flow, assets, liabilities, and the power of compounding. By gaining a comprehensive understanding of these concepts, individuals can make more informed decisions about their finances and investment strategies.

Building Financial Literacy: Kiyosaki advocates for developing financial literacy, which involves acquiring knowledge and skills related to managing personal finances. This includes budgeting, saving, debt management, and understanding the impact of financial decisions. By improving financial literacy, individuals can make smarter choices and avoid common pitfalls that hinder financial progress.

Learning from Experts: Kiyosaki encourages individuals to learn from experts in the field of finance and investing. This can involve reading books, attending seminars, listening to podcasts, or seeking mentorship from experienced investors. Learning from those who have achieved financial success can provide valuable insights and guidance on building wealth effectively.

Expanding Investment Knowledge: Kiyosaki advises individuals to continuously expand their knowledge about different investment options and strategies. This includes learning about stocks, bonds, real estate, business ownership, and other investment vehicles. By broadening their investment knowledge, individuals can make more informed decisions and identify opportunities that align with their financial goals.

Analyzing Market Trends: Kiyosaki emphasizes the importance of staying informed about market trends and economic indicators. This involves understanding how various factors, such as interest rates, inflation, and geopolitical events, can impact investments. By analyzing market trends, individuals can make more informed investment decisions and adjust their strategies accordingly.

Risk Management: Kiyosaki stresses the need to understand and manage investment risks effectively. This involves learning about different types of risks, such as market risk, credit risk, and liquidity risk, and implementing risk management strategies. By having a solid understanding of risk, individuals can make informed decisions and protect their capital.

Developing a Growth Mindset: Kiyosaki believes that a growth mindset is essential for continuous learning and improvement. By adopting a mindset that embraces challenges, seeks new knowledge, and embraces feedback, individuals can continue to expand their financial education and adapt to changing market conditions.

By prioritizing financial education, individuals can gain the knowledge and skills necessary to make sound financial decisions and achieve their financial goals. Robert Kiyosaki's emphasis on financial education highlights the importance of acquiring a strong foundation of financial literacy, continuously expanding investment knowledge, and developing a growth mindset. By investing in their financial education, individuals can enhance their ability to navigate the world of finance, build wealth, and attain financial independence.

Invest for Cash Flow

Robert Kiyosaki stresses the importance of investing for cash flow as a key strategy for building wealth and achieving financial independence. Kiyosaki's philosophy revolves around acquiring income-generating assets that provide a consistent stream of cash flow over time. Here are further insights into the implications of Kiyosaki's emphasis on investing for cash flow:

Focus on Passive Income: Kiyosaki advocates for investing in assets that generate passive income. These can include rental properties, dividend-paying stocks, bonds, or businesses that produce regular income. By prioritizing investments that generate cash flow, individuals can create a reliable source of income that is independent of their active involvement.

Cash Flow vs. Capital Gains: Kiyosaki distinguishes between cash flow and capital gains. While capital gains refer to the increase in the value of an asset over time, cash flow represents the ongoing income generated by the asset. Kiyosaki emphasizes the importance of prioritizing cash flow over capital gains, as cash flow provides a steady income stream that can support financial goals and lifestyle.

Sustainable Income: Investing for cash flow allows individuals to create a sustainable income source. By focusing on assets that consistently generate positive cash flow, individuals can cover their expenses, reinvest for further growth, and achieve financial stability. Sustainable income provides financial security and the freedom to pursue personal goals and passions.

Diversification of Cash Flow: Kiyosaki encourages diversifying cash flow sources to minimize risk and enhance financial stability. By investing in a variety of income-generating assets, individuals can spread their risk across different industries and mitigate the impact of potential downturns in specific sectors. Diversification of cash flow helps protect against volatility and ensures a more resilient financial position.

Investing for the Long Term: Kiyosaki's approach to investing for cash flow aligns with a long-term perspective. He advises investors to adopt a patient mindset and focus on the sustainable income potential of their investments. By prioritizing long-term cash flow generation, individuals can benefit from the compounding effect of reinvesting income over time.

Risk Management: Kiyosaki emphasizes the importance of risk management when investing for cash flow. This involves conducting thorough due diligence, analyzing investment opportunities, and understanding the potential risks associated with different assets. By carefully managing risk, individuals can protect their capital and ensure the sustainability of their cash flow investments.

Financial Independence: Investing for cash flow aligns with Kiyosaki's vision of achieving financial independence. By generating passive income that exceeds expenses, individuals can free themselves from financial constraints and gain the flexibility to pursue their desired lifestyle. Cash flow-focused investments provide the means to attain financial independence and the freedom to live life on one's own terms.

This approach prioritizes sustainable income over capital gains, encourages diversification, and aligns with long-term financial goals. By focusing on cash flow, individuals can create a reliable source of income, achieve financial independence, and ultimately enjoy greater financial freedom and security.

Investment Isn't Risky

Robert Kiyosaki challenges the commonly held belief that investment is inherently risky. He believes that investment itself is not risky but rather the lack of financial education and understanding of investment principles that pose the real risk. Kiyosaki encourages individuals to acquire the necessary knowledge and skills to make informed investment decisions, thereby minimizing the perceived risks. Here are further insights into the implications of Kiyosaki's viewpoint:

Risk Mitigation through Education: Kiyosaki argues that the key to reducing investment risks is to invest in one's financial education. By gaining a deep understanding of investment principles, financial markets, and different asset classes, individuals can make informed decisions and mitigate potential risks. The more knowledgeable one becomes, the better equipped they are to navigate the complexities of investing.

Diversification and Risk Management: Kiyosaki emphasizes the importance of diversification and risk management in investment. By diversifying investments across various asset classes, industries, and geographical locations, individuals can spread their risk and reduce exposure to any single investment. Additionally, implementing risk management strategies, such as setting stop-loss orders or using asset allocation techniques, can further minimize potential risks.

Long-Term Perspective: Kiyosaki advocates for adopting a long-term perspective when it comes to investment. He believes that short-term market fluctuations and volatility should not deter individuals from their investment goals. By focusing on long-term trends, fundamentals, and the potential for compounding returns, individuals can weather short-term market fluctuations and potentially achieve significant gains over time.

Opportunity Cost: Kiyosaki highlights the concept of opportunity cost when considering investment risks. He argues that the real risk lies in not taking action and missing out on potential opportunities for growth and wealth creation. By staying on the sidelines and not investing, individuals may miss out on the potential returns that investments can offer.

Embracing Mistakes as Learning Opportunities: Kiyosaki encourages individuals to view mistakes and failures as learning opportunities rather than as setbacks. He believes that it is through learning from mistakes and adapting strategies that individuals can grow as investors and ultimately reduce risks. By embracing a growth mindset and learning from past experiences, individuals can improve their investment decision-making abilities.

Risk-Reward Trade-Off: Kiyosaki acknowledges that there is always a certain level of risk associated with investing. However, he emphasizes the importance of understanding the risk-reward trade-off. Higher potential returns often come with higher risks, and individuals need to assess their risk tolerance and align it with their investment objectives. By carefully evaluating potential returns against the associated risks, individuals can make informed investment decisions that suit their risk appetite.

While no investment is entirely risk-free, Robert Kiyosaki challenges the notion that investment itself is inherently risky. He believes that risks can be minimized through education, diversification, risk management, and a long-term perspective. By acquiring financial knowledge and developing sound investment strategies, individuals can navigate the investment landscape with greater confidence and potentially achieve their financial goals while managing risks effectively.

Raise Capital

Robert Kiyosaki emphasizes the importance of raising capital as a crucial aspect of building wealth and achieving financial success. Kiyosaki believes that having access to sufficient capital is instrumental in pursuing investment opportunities, starting businesses, and creating financial independence. Here are further insights into the implications of Kiyosaki's viewpoint on raising capital:

Expand Investment Opportunities: Kiyosaki highlights that raising capital provides individuals with the means to discover a wider range of investment opportunities. With sufficient capital at their disposal, individuals can consider ventures that may require significant upfront investments or have the potential for higher returns. Raising capital enables investors to capitalize on lucrative opportunities that align with their investment goals.

Leverage Other People's Money: Kiyosaki encourages individuals to leverage other people's money, such as loans or investment partnerships, to raise capital. By strategically utilizing borrowed funds or pooling resources with others, individuals can amplify their investment power and take advantage of opportunities that may have been out of reach otherwise. Leverage allows for the expansion of investment portfolios and potentially increases returns.

Start or Expand Businesses: Raising capital is often essential for starting or expanding businesses. Entrepreneurs require capital to finance business operations, purchase assets, hire employees, and drive growth. By raising capital, individuals can fund their entrepreneurial endeavors and increase the chances of building successful enterprises that generate sustainable income and long-term wealth.

Network and Build Relationships: Kiyosaki emphasizes that raising capital often involves networking and building relationships with potential investors or lenders. Developing strong relationships in the business and investment community opens doors to capital sources and opportunities. By actively networking and cultivating relationships, individuals can access a broader pool of capital providers and increase their chances of securing the funding they need.

Financial Education and Presentation: Kiyosaki highlights the significance of financial education and effective presentation skills when raising capital. Investors and lenders need to have confidence in the individual or business seeking capital. Presenting a compelling business case, demonstrating a solid understanding of financials, and articulating investment opportunities can enhance credibility and attract potential capital providers.

Risk Management: Kiyosaki emphasizes the need for careful risk management when raising capital. While access to capital can provide opportunities, it also comes with responsibility. Individuals need to assess their risk tolerance, thoroughly evaluate potential investments, and develop strategies to manage risks associated with capital utilization. Effective risk management helps protect the capital raised and maximize the chances of achieving positive investment outcomes.

Continuous Improvement: Kiyosaki highlights the importance of continuous improvement and adapting to feedback when raising capital. Investors and lenders often evaluate the track record, performance, and growth potential of individuals or businesses seeking capital. By continually improving one's financial knowledge, refining investment strategies, and demonstrating a commitment to growth, individuals can enhance their credibility and increase their chances of successfully raising capital.

Raising capital plays a vital role in creating investment opportunities, starting or expanding businesses, and building wealth. Robert Kiyosaki emphasizes the significance of accessing sufficient capital and leveraging it effectively to pursue financial goals. By expanding investment opportunities, networking, acquiring financial knowledge, and managing risks, individuals can enhance their ability to raise capital and unlock the potential for greater financial success.

Chapter 5: The Steve Jobs Strategies

STEVE JOBS (1955-2011) was an American entrepreneur, business magnate, and inventor who co-founded Apple Inc. and played a pivotal role in revolutionizing the technology industry. With his visionary leadership and passion for design, Jobs transformed multiple industries, including personal computers, smartphones, digital music, and animation. His innovative products, such as the Macintosh, iPhone, iPod, and iPad, have had a profound impact on the way people live, work, and communicate.

Jobs' remarkable journey is characterized by his relentless pursuit of excellence, emphasis on user-friendly design, and uncompromising attention to detail.

Jobs was known for his extraordinary vision and ability to anticipate future trends. He had an innate sense of what consumers wanted even before they knew it themselves. Jobs had a remarkable talent for identifying gaps in the market and creating products that captured people's imagination.

One of Jobs' greatest strengths was his focus on creating beautifully designed, user-friendly products. He believed in the importance of combining technology with elegance and simplicity, leading to the development of groundbreaking devices that revolutionized industries.

Jobs famously stated, "Simplicity is the ultimate sophistication." He had a keen eye for minimalistic design and believed in eliminating unnecessary complexity. By focusing on simplicity, Jobs made technology accessible to a wider audience and changed the way people interact with devices.

He had an exceptional ability to create excitement around new products, build a loyal customer base, and position Apple as a brand synonymous with innovation and high-quality user experiences.

Jobs encountered numerous setbacks throughout his career, including being ousted from Apple in 1985. However, he remained resilient and returned to the company in 1997, leading it to unprecedented success. His determination, unwavering focus, and refusal to give up played a crucial role in his eventual triumphs.

Jobs had exacting standards for every aspect of Apple's products, from hardware to software and even packaging. He demanded excellence and pushed his teams to deliver the best possible user experience. This obsession with quality and attention to detail set Apple apart from its competitors.

Steve Jobs' impact on the technology industry and popular culture cannot be overstated. His innovative products and visionary leadership continue to shape the world we live in today. His legacy serves as an inspiration for entrepreneurs, designers, and dreamers worldwide, encouraging them to think differently and challenge the status quo.

Although Steve Jobs passed away in 2011, his influence remains strong, and his contributions to the world of technology and design continue to shape our lives. His ability to blend technology, art, and business acumen has left an indelible mark on the world, making him one of the most influential figures of our time.

Follow Your Passion

Steve Jobs famously encouraged individuals to follow their passion. He believed that pursuing one's passion was essential for finding fulfillment and achieving extraordinary success. Here are further insights into the implications of Steve Jobs' emphasis on following one's passion:

Discovering Purpose: Jobs believed that following one's passion helps individuals discover their true purpose in life. By identifying what truly inspires and motivates them, individuals can align their personal and professional pursuits with their core values and interests. This alignment fosters a sense of purpose and fuels the drive to excel.

Overcoming Challenges: Passion provides the inner fuel needed to overcome challenges and persevere in the face of obstacles. When individuals are passionate about what they do, they are more likely to push through setbacks, take risks, and persist until they achieve their goals. Passion acts as a powerful motivator during challenging times and helps individuals maintain focus and resilience.

Enhancing Creativity: Following one's passion often taps into a person's innate creativity. When individuals engage in activities they are passionate about, they are more likely to think creatively, challenge conventional norms, and come up with innovative solutions. Passion fuels imagination and encourages individuals to discover new possibilities.

Sustained Motivation: Passion provides a continuous source of motivation and energy. When individuals are passionate about their work or projects, they are more likely to be self-driven, intrinsically motivated, and willing to put in the necessary effort to excel. Passion fuels a sense of purpose, leading to a higher level of engagement and dedication.

Pursuing Excellence: Steve Jobs believed that passion was the key to achieving excellence. When individuals are deeply passionate about what they do, they strive for perfection and go above and beyond to deliver exceptional results. Passion drives individuals to continuously improve their skills, knowledge, and abilities, leading to mastery in their chosen field.

Inspiring Others: Following one's passion has the potential to inspire and influence others. When individuals pursue their passions with enthusiasm and dedication, they become role models and encourage others to follow their own dreams. Passion is contagious, and it has the power to create a ripple effect, inspiring positive change in individuals and communities.

Personal Fulfillment: Ultimately, following one's passion leads to personal fulfillment and a sense of contentment. When individuals engage in activities that align with their passions, they experience a deep sense of satisfaction and happiness. This fulfillment extends beyond material success and contributes to overall well-being and a fulfilling life.

Steve Jobs' emphasis on following one's passion serves as a reminder for individuals to pursue what truly ignites their hearts and drives their enthusiasm. By aligning personal and professional pursuits with their passions, individuals can tap into their full potential, overcome challenges, and create a life that is both meaningful and fulfilling. Following one's passion is not only a pathway to individual success but also a way to make a positive impact on the world.

Say No to a Thousand Things, Keep Your Focus

Steve Jobs emphasized the importance of focus and the ability to say no to distractions. He believed that maintaining a clear focus was key to achieving excellence and making significant contributions. Here are further insights into the implications of Jobs' advice to "say no to a thousand things" and keep one's focus:

Prioritization: Jobs encouraged individuals to prioritize their efforts and be selective in their pursuits. By saying no to various distractions and opportunities that do not align with their core goals, individuals can focus their time and energy on the most important tasks and projects. This prioritization ensures that valuable resources are allocated effectively.

Simplification: Saying no to a thousand things allows individuals to simplify their lives and avoid unnecessary complexities. By eliminating distractions, individuals can streamline their focus and dedicate their attention to the essential aspects of their work or projects. Simplification promotes clarity and enables individuals to make more meaningful contributions.

Concentrated Effort: Jobs believed in the power of concentrated effort. By focusing on a limited number of projects or ideas, individuals can channel their energy and expertise more effectively. This concentrated effort enhances productivity and the quality of work, leading to greater impact and success.

Quality Over Quantity: Jobs emphasized the importance of quality over quantity. By saying no to a multitude of things, individuals can devote more time and attention to fewer projects or ideas, ensuring a higher standard of execution. This commitment to quality sets individuals apart and allows them to create meaningful and influential contributions.

Avoiding Distractions: Distractions can derail progress and hinder focus. Jobs recognized the need to resist the allure of distractions and stay dedicated to the task at hand. By saying no to distractions, individuals can maintain a clear focus and maximize their productivity and creativity.

Making Strategic Decisions: Saying no to a thousand things is a strategic decision-making process. It requires individuals to assess opportunities and commitments, align them with their goals and values, and make intentional choices. By making strategic decisions about where to invest time and resources, individuals can pursue the most promising and impactful endeavors.

Achieving Excellence: Jobs believed that maintaining focus was essential for achieving excellence. By saying no to distractions and keeping one's focus on the most important areas, individuals can concentrate their efforts and strive for mastery. This dedication to excellence leads to remarkable achievements and sets individuals apart from the average.

Steve Jobs' advice to "say no to a thousand things" and keep one's focus underscores the importance of prioritization, simplification, and concentrated effort. By avoiding distractions and making strategic decisions about where to invest time and resources, individuals can achieve excellence and create a lasting impact in their chosen pursuits. Maintaining focus is a key ingredient for success in a world filled with countless opportunities and distractions.

Don't be Scared by Death

Steve Jobs famously addressed the topic of death and its impact on one's perspective and approach to life. He believed that the awareness of mortality could be a catalyst for living a purposeful and meaningful life. Here are further insights into the implications of Jobs' advice to not be scared by death:

Seizing Opportunities: Acknowledging the finite nature of life can inspire individuals to seize opportunities and make the most of their time. By realizing that life is transient, individuals may be motivated to pursue their passions, take risks, and embrace new experiences without fear or hesitation.

Living Authentically: Jobs' message encourages individuals to live authentically and true to themselves. The awareness of mortality can prompt introspection and reflection, leading individuals to prioritize what truly matters to them. By aligning their actions with their values and passions, individuals can lead a more fulfilling and purpose-driven life.

Overcoming Fear: The fear of death often permeates many aspects of life, holding individuals back from taking risks and pursuing their dreams. Jobs' perspective encourages individuals to confront their fear of death and embrace it as a reminder to live fully. By embracing mortality, individuals can free themselves from the shackles of fear and approach life with courage and resilience.

Focus on Legacy: The contemplation of death can prompt individuals to reflect on their legacy and the impact they want to leave behind. Jobs believed in leaving a lasting legacy through the work one does and the contributions made to society. By considering the impact they want to make, individuals can strive to create a positive and enduring influence on the world.

Gratitude and Mindfulness: The awareness of mortality can foster a sense of gratitude and mindfulness in individuals. Jobs encouraged individuals to appreciate the present moment and be mindful of the preciousness of life. By practicing gratitude and mindfulness, individuals can derive more joy from everyday experiences and cultivate a deeper appreciation for the people and things around them.

Embracing Change: Jobs' perspective on death also underscores the inevitability of change. The awareness of life's impermanence can help individuals navigate change and adapt to new circumstances with resilience. By embracing change and letting go of attachments, individuals can embrace personal growth and find new opportunities for fulfillment.

Steve Jobs' advice to not be scared by death encourages individuals to confront their mortality and use it as a catalyst for living a purposeful and meaningful life. By embracing the transient nature of life, individuals can seize opportunities, live authentically, overcome fear, focus on their legacy, practice gratitude and mindfulness, and embrace change. Jobs' perspective serves as a reminder to appreciate the present moment and make the most of the time we have.

Identify With the Kings, to Get the Kings Honor

The statement "Identify with the kings, to get the king's honor" refers to the idea of aligning oneself with successful and accomplished individuals in order to achieve similar levels of success and recognition. While this quote is not directly attributed to Steve Jobs, it reflects a mindset that he and other successful individuals have embraced throughout their careers. Here are some insights into the implications of this perspective:

Surrounding Yourself with Excellence: To achieve greatness, it can be beneficial to surround yourself with individuals who have already achieved what you aspire to. By associating with successful and accomplished individuals, you can learn from their experiences, gain insights into their strategies, and be inspired by their achievements. Their mindset and approach can provide valuable lessons and serve as a source of motivation.

Learning from Role Models: Identifying with those who have attained high levels of success allows you to learn from their behaviors, habits, and decision-making processes. By observing and studying the qualities and strategies that have contributed to their success, you can adopt similar principles and apply them to your own endeavors. This can help you avoid pitfalls, make informed choices, and increase your chances of achieving honorable outcomes.

Building a Supportive Network: Aligning yourself with successful individuals can also help you build a supportive network. Surrounding yourself with accomplished individuals who share similar values and goals can provide a support system that can propel you forward. This network can offer guidance, collaboration opportunities, and a sense of accountability, all of which can contribute to your personal and professional growth.

Shifting Your Mindset: Identifying with successful individuals can influence your mindset and help you adopt a more success-oriented approach. By studying the mindset and attitudes of those who have achieved significant success, you can develop a similar mindset that is focused on growth, resilience, and continuous improvement. This shift in mindset can positively impact your actions, decisions, and overall trajectory.

Raising your Standards: Being surrounded by accomplished individuals can elevate your own standards and expectations. By observing the level of excellence achieved by those you identify with, you may be motivated to set higher goals and strive for greater achievements. This can push you to stretch beyond your comfort zone and unlock your full potential.

Seeking Mentorship: Identifying with successful individuals can open doors to mentorship opportunities. Establishing a mentor-mentee relationship with someone who has achieved the level of success you aspire to can provide invaluable guidance, advice, and support. Having a mentor can accelerate your learning, help you navigate challenges, and offer insights that can accelerate your growth.

While the quote may not be directly from Steve Jobs, the concept of identifying with successful individuals to achieve similar recognition and honor is a mindset embraced by many accomplished individuals. By aligning yourself with those who have achieved excellence, learning from their experiences, and adopting their mindset and strategies, you can increase your chances of achieving your own version of success and earning the respect and recognition you desire.

Surround Yourself With Great Players

STEVE JOBS BELIEVED in the power of surrounding oneself with great players, referring to talented and high-performing individuals. He recognized the importance of building a strong team and fostering an environment where talented individuals could collaborate and excel together. Here are further insights into the implications of Jobs' advice to surround yourself with great players:

Synergy and Collaboration: Jobs understood that great players thrive in an environment where they can collaborate and leverage each other's strengths. By surrounding oneself with talented individuals, there is an opportunity to create synergy, where the collective efforts and skills of the team result in outcomes greater than the sum of their individual contributions. Collaboration fosters innovation, creativity, and collective problem-solving.

High Standards and Accountability: When surrounded by great players, there is a natural elevation of standards and expectations. Talented individuals often push each other to excel and hold each other accountable for delivering exceptional results. This fosters a culture of continuous improvement and ensures that the team remains focused on achieving excellence in their work.

Learning and Growth: Being surrounded by great players offers ample opportunities for learning and personal growth. Interacting with talented individuals provides exposure to new perspectives, ideas, and approaches. It allows for knowledge sharing, skill development, and professional growth through observing and learning from the expertise of others.

Complementary Skills and Expertise: Great players often possess diverse skill sets and expertise. When working together, they can complement each other's strengths and compensate for each other's weaknesses. This creates a dynamic and well-rounded team capable of tackling complex challenges from multiple angles and finding innovative solutions.

Motivation and Inspiration: Surrounding oneself with great players can be highly motivating and inspiring. Being in the presence of talented individuals who are passionate about their work and constantly striving for excellence can ignite one's own motivation and drive. Great players can serve as role models, pushing others to raise their own standards and reach new heights.

Creating a Positive Culture: The presence of great players contributes to the development of a positive and high-performing team culture. Their collective commitment to excellence, collaboration, and continuous improvement sets the tone for the entire team. This positive culture fosters innovation, employee engagement, and a sense of collective purpose.

Increased Potential for Success: Surrounding oneself with great players increases the potential for success. The collective capabilities, skills, and determination of a team of talented individuals can propel projects forward, overcome obstacles, and achieve remarkable results. With a team of great players, there is a higher likelihood of reaching ambitious goals and achieving extraordinary success.

Steve Jobs' advice to surround oneself with great players underscores the importance of teamwork, collaboration, and the positive impact that talented individuals can have on overall performance and success. By building a team of exceptional individuals, one can foster a culture of excellence, continuous improvement, and collective achievement, ultimately driving innovation and accomplishing remarkable outcomes.

When Life Hit You, Fire Back

"When life hits you first, fire back" reflects a resilient mindset that encourages individuals to respond to life's challenges and setbacks with determination and perseverance. Although this quote is not directly attributed to Steve Jobs, it aligns with his philosophy of resilience and overcoming adversity. Here are further insights into the implications of this perspective:

Resilience in the Face of Adversity: Life is full of ups and downs, and setbacks are inevitable. The quote encourages individuals to respond to life's challenges with resilience, refusing to let adversity define them. Instead of succumbing to difficulties, individuals are encouraged to gather their strength, learn from the experience, and use it as fuel to overcome obstacles.

Taking Control of Circumstances: "Firing back" implies taking control of one's circumstances rather than passively accepting them. It emphasizes the importance of proactive action in the face of adversity. Instead of allowing challenges to dictate the course of life, individuals are encouraged to take charge, make empowered decisions, and navigate through obstacles with determination.

Embracing a Positive Mindset: The quote encourages individuals to adopt a positive mindset even in challenging situations. It promotes the idea of viewing setbacks as opportunities for growth, learning, and personal development. By reframing adversity as a catalyst for improvement, individuals can maintain a positive outlook and persevere through difficult times.

Learning from Setbacks: Adversity often presents valuable lessons. The quote encourages individuals to extract wisdom and insights from challenging experiences. By reflecting on setbacks, individuals can gain valuable knowledge that can inform future decision-making, improve strategies, and enhance personal development.

Taking Bold and Decisive Action: "Firing back" implies a proactive and assertive response to life's challenges. It encourages individuals to take bold and decisive action rather than passively accepting defeat. By responding with determination and courage, individuals can regain control, overcome obstacles, and make progress towards their goals.

Building Inner Strength: The quote highlights the importance of building inner strength and resilience. Adversity can test one's character and resolve. By firing back and facing challenges head-on, individuals can develop the inner fortitude necessary to withstand life's trials and emerge stronger on the other side.

Cultivating Perseverance: The quote emphasizes the significance of perseverance in the face of adversity. It encourages individuals not to give up but to persist in their pursuit of success. By persevering through challenges, individuals can build resilience, achieve personal growth, and ultimately reach their desired outcomes.

While the quote may not be directly attributed to Steve Jobs, it reflects a mindset aligned with his belief in resilience and the ability to overcome obstacles. By firing back in the face of adversity, individuals can cultivate resilience, take control of their circumstances, and navigate life's challenges with determination and perseverance.

Demand the Best from People

Steve Jobs believed in demanding the best from people as a means to bring out their full potential and achieve exceptional outcomes. He emphasized the importance of setting high standards and challenging individuals to reach their highest level of performance. Here are further insights into the implications of Jobs' perspective on demanding the best from people:

Inspiring Excellence: Jobs believed that by demanding the best from people, individuals are inspired to push their boundaries and strive for excellence. Setting high expectations encourages individuals to rise to the challenge, tap into their capabilities, and deliver their best work. Jobs' approach aimed to unlock the untapped potential within individuals and teams.

Creating a Culture of Excellence: By demanding the best, Jobs sought to create a culture where excellence became the norm. When high standards are consistently expected and maintained, they become ingrained in the organization's DNA. Demanding the best fosters a culture of continuous improvement, where individuals are motivated to innovate, problem-solve, and raise their performance to new levels.

Stretching Limits: Jobs believed in pushing people beyond their comfort zones to achieve extraordinary results. By demanding the best, individuals are compelled to stretch their limits and surpass their perceived capabilities. This mindset encourages personal and professional growth, leading to breakthroughs and achievements that were previously deemed impossible.

Accountability and Responsibility: Demanding the best holds individuals accountable for their actions and outcomes. Jobs believed in fostering a sense of responsibility and ownership among team members. By setting high expectations, individuals are motivated to take ownership of their work, be accountable for results, and continuously strive for improvement.

Fostering Innovation: Jobs understood that demanding the best from people fosters a climate of innovation. By challenging individuals to go beyond their comfort zones and push the boundaries of what is possible, creativity and innovation are sparked. Demanding excellence encourages individuals to think outside the box, discover new ideas, and find innovative solutions to complex problems.

Building Trust and Confidence: Demanding the best from people demonstrates a belief in their capabilities. When individuals feel that their leaders and colleagues have confidence in their abilities, it fosters trust and boosts self-confidence. This trust and confidence can inspire individuals to take risks, embrace challenges, and deliver exceptional results.

Attracting and Retaining Top Talent: By demanding the best, Jobs aimed to attract and retain top talent. Talented individuals are often drawn to challenging environments that allow them to showcase their skills and reach their full potential. Jobs' approach to demanding excellence created an environment where high performers thrived and were motivated to contribute their best work.

Steve Jobs' belief in demanding the best from people reflects his drive for excellence and his desire to create exceptional products and experiences. By setting high expectations, fostering a culture of continuous improvement, and challenging individuals to exceed their perceived limits, Jobs aimed to bring out the best in people and achieve extraordinary results. Demanding excellence not only drives individual and organizational success but also inspires innovation, fosters personal growth, and creates a culture of continuous improvement.

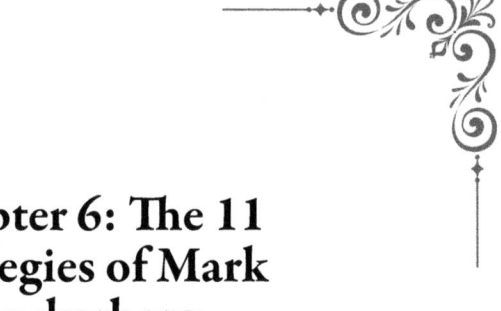

Chapter 6: The 11 Strategies of Mark Zuckerberg

MARK ZUCKERBERG IS an American technology entrepreneur and the co-founder of Facebook, one of the world's largest social media platforms. Born in 1984, Zuckerberg demonstrated a passion for computer programming from an early age. While studying at Harvard University, he launched Facebook in 2004 with his college roommates, Eduardo Saverin, Andrew McCollum, Dustin Moskovitz, and Chris Hughes.

Zuckerberg's vision for Facebook was to create a platform that connects people and enables them to share and communicate with each other online. What started as a social networking site for Harvard students quickly expanded to other universities and eventually opened up to the public, reaching billions of users worldwide.

MARK ZUCKERBERG EMBODIES the entrepreneurial spirit, demonstrating a relentless drive to turn ideas into reality. From the inception of Facebook in his Harvard dorm room to its transformation into a global phenomenon, Zuckerberg's entrepreneurial journey showcases his ambition, determination, and innovative thinking.

Zuckerberg's vision for Facebook centered around connecting people and facilitating communication. He recognized the power of social connections and the potential for technology to bring individuals closer together, transcending geographical boundaries and cultural barriers. Through Facebook, he revolutionized how people interact and share information in the digital age.

Emphasis on User Experience: Zuckerberg prioritizes user experience, constantly refining and evolving Facebook's features to enhance usability and engagement. He understands the importance of providing a seamless and intuitive platform that users find valuable and enjoyable. This focus on user experience has been instrumental in Facebook's widespread adoption and ongoing success.

Zuckerberg has consistently pushed the boundaries of innovation, expanding Facebook's capabilities beyond a mere social networking site. Under his leadership, Facebook has acquired several companies, including Instagram and WhatsApp, broadening its reach and diversifying its services. He has also discoverd emerging technologies such as virtual reality and artificial intelligence to shape the future of social interaction.

Alongside his entrepreneurial pursuits, Zuckerberg is actively engaged in philanthropy. Together with his wife, Priscilla Chan, he established the Chan Zuckerberg Initiative, a charitable organization focused on advancing human potential and equality. Through this initiative, he has committed significant resources to various causes, including education, healthcare, and scientific research.

Zuckerberg has faced challenges related to privacy and data security concerns on the Facebook platform. In response, he has taken steps to improve privacy controls, increase transparency, and address issues related to user data protection. He continues to emphasize the importance of safeguarding user privacy while maintaining an open and connected online community.

Zuckerberg maintains a long-term perspective when it comes to Facebook's growth and impact. He envisions Facebook as a platform that connects individuals, fosters communities, and drives positive social change. His commitment to this vision is evident in his strategic decisions, product development, and ongoing efforts to address societal issues through the platform.

Mark Zuckerberg's leadership and innovation have made an indelible mark on the technology and social media landscape. His entrepreneurial spirit, focus on connectivity, emphasis on user experience, and commitment to social impact have shaped Facebook into a global phenomenon. Zuckerberg continues to navigate the challenges and opportunities that arise in the ever-evolving digital landscape, striving to create a more connected and inclusive world through his ongoing efforts with Facebook and philanthropic initiatives.

Have a Dream

Mark Zuckerberg encourages individuals to have a dream, reflecting his belief in the power of ambitious goals and aspirations. By having a dream, individuals can fuel their motivation, shape their actions, and work towards achieving their vision. Here are further insights into the implications of Zuckerberg's emphasis on having a dream:

Vision and Purpose: Having a dream provides individuals with a clear vision and purpose. It helps define the direction they want to pursue in their personal or professional lives. A dream serves as a guiding light, inspiring individuals to set goals and make decisions aligned with their aspirations.

Motivation and Ambition: Dreams fuel motivation and ambition. When individuals have a compelling vision, they are more likely to be driven to take action, overcome obstacles, and persist in the face of challenges. A dream gives individuals a sense of purpose and a reason to push beyond their comfort zones.

Goal Setting: Having a dream allows individuals to set specific, meaningful goals that align with their overarching vision. Dreams provide a framework for setting milestones and breaking down larger aspirations into actionable steps. By setting goals, individuals can track progress and make progress towards their ultimate vision.

Innovation and Creativity: Dreams inspire innovation and creativity. When individuals have a dream, they are encouraged to think outside the box, challenge conventional thinking, and come up with novel solutions. Dreams provide a canvas for individuals to discover new possibilities and unleash their creative potential.

Resilience and Perseverance: Pursuing a dream requires resilience and perseverance. Challenges and setbacks are inevitable, but having a dream provides individuals with the determination to weather those storms. The belief in the dream acts as a driving force, enabling individuals to bounce back from failures and keep moving forward.

Continuous Growth: Dreams foster personal growth and development. The pursuit of a dream often requires individuals to acquire new skills, gain knowledge, and expand their horizons. Having a dream motivates individuals to seek opportunities for growth, embrace learning experiences, and evolve as they work towards their vision.

Inspiring Others: Having a dream can inspire others to pursue their own aspirations. When individuals share their dreams and demonstrate their commitment to achieving them, they become a source of inspiration for those around them. Dreams have the power to ignite passion and encourage others to strive for greatness.

Mark Zuckerberg's encouragement to have a dream reflects his belief in the transformative power of ambitious aspirations. By embracing a dream, individuals can harness motivation, set meaningful goals, foster innovation, build resilience, and inspire others. Dreams serve as a compass that guides individuals on their journey towards personal fulfillment and making a positive impact on the world.

Start Small

Mark Zuckerberg advocates for starting small, emphasizing the importance of taking initial steps and making progress towards one's goals. By starting small, individuals can overcome barriers, gain momentum, and gradually build towards bigger achievements. Here are further insights into the implications of Zuckerberg's advice to start small:

Overcoming Paralysis: Starting small helps individuals overcome the paralysis that can come from facing overwhelming goals or projects. Breaking a larger goal into smaller, manageable tasks makes the overall endeavor more approachable and less daunting. It allows individuals to take that crucial first step without feeling overwhelmed by the magnitude of the entire undertaking.

Building Momentum: Starting small enables individuals to build momentum and gain confidence. Accomplishing smaller tasks or milestones early on creates a positive feedback loop that fuels motivation and encourages continued progress. This momentum can propel individuals forward, increasing their likelihood of reaching more significant achievements over time.

Learning through Iteration: Starting small allows for an iterative process of learning and improvement. By initiating smaller projects or experiments, individuals can gather valuable insights, identify areas for growth, and make adjustments along the way. This iterative approach enables individuals to refine their strategies and increase their chances of success as they progress.

Testing and Validating Ideas: Starting small provides an opportunity to test and validate ideas before committing significant resources or effort. By beginning with a smaller scale, individuals can gauge market response, gather feedback, and make informed decisions about the viability of their ideas. This iterative testing process allows for adjustments and refinements, increasing the likelihood of long-term success.

Cultivating a Growth Mindset: Starting small fosters a growth mindset, emphasizing the value of continuous learning and improvement. It encourages individuals to embrace challenges, see setbacks as opportunities for growth, and persist despite initial obstacles. This mindset promotes resilience, adaptability, and a willingness to take calculated risks in pursuit of larger goals.

Building a Strong Foundation: Starting small enables individuals to build a solid foundation for future growth. By focusing on fundamental skills, gaining practical experience, and mastering the essentials, individuals can develop a strong base upon which they can later expand and tackle more significant challenges. Starting small lays the groundwork for long-term success and sustainability.

Scaling Up Gradually: Starting small allows for gradual scaling and expansion. By initially focusing on a smaller scope, individuals can refine their processes, systems, and capabilities before taking on larger endeavors. This incremental growth approach mitigates risks, ensures stability, and increases the likelihood of sustainable long-term success.

Mark Zuckerberg's emphasis on starting small highlights the importance of taking action, embracing learning, and building momentum. By beginning with manageable steps and gradually scaling up, individuals can overcome challenges, refine their strategies, and ultimately achieve significant accomplishments. Starting small sets the foundation for sustained progress and long-term success in both personal and professional pursuits.

Believe in Yourself

Believing in oneself is a fundamental principle advocated by many successful individuals, including Mark Zuckerberg. It reflects the importance of self-confidence, self-belief, and a positive mindset in achieving personal and professional goals. Here are further insights into the implications of believing in oneself:

Self-Confidence: Believing in yourself cultivates self-confidence, which is vital for success. When you believe in your abilities and value, you approach challenges with a sense of assurance and resilience. Self-confidence allows you to navigate obstacles, take calculated risks, and persevere in the face of setbacks.

Overcoming Self-Doubt: Belief in oneself helps to overcome self-doubt and insecurities. It allows you to challenge negative thoughts, embrace your strengths, and recognize your potential. By acknowledging your worth and capabilities, you can counteract self-limiting beliefs and move forward with conviction.

Resilience and Perseverance: Believing in yourself fuels resilience and perseverance. When faced with challenges or failures, a strong self-belief system helps you bounce back, learn from setbacks, and maintain a positive mindset. Believing in your abilities and potential keeps you motivated and committed to achieving your goals.

Embracing Opportunities: Belief in oneself opens doors to embracing opportunities. When you have confidence in your skills and talents, you are more likely to seize new opportunities that come your way. Believing in yourself gives you the courage to step outside your comfort zone, take on new challenges, and discover uncharted territories.

Positive Mindset: Believing in yourself fosters a positive mindset. Positive self-belief influences your thoughts, emotions, and actions, enabling you to approach situations with optimism and a can-do attitude. A positive mindset attracts opportunities, fosters resilience, and enhances overall well-being.

Setting Higher Goals: Belief in oneself empowers you to set higher goals and aspirations. When you believe in your ability to accomplish great things, you aim for ambitious targets and push beyond your perceived limits. Belief in yourself fuels motivation and encourages you to strive for personal and professional growth.

Inspiring Others: Believing in yourself can inspire others to do the same. When you demonstrate confidence, determination, and self-assurance, you become a role model for others. Your belief in yourself can inspire those around you to embrace their own capabilities and pursue their dreams.

Believing in yourself is a cornerstone for personal and professional success. It empowers you to overcome challenges, seize opportunities, and strive for excellence. By cultivating a strong self-belief system, you can tap into your full potential, foster resilience, and inspire others to do the same. Remember, your belief in yourself is a powerful force that can shape your journey and help you achieve remarkable things.

Follow Your Passion

Following your passion is a mantra often shared by successful individuals, emphasizing the importance of pursuing what genuinely excites and motivates you. It encourages individuals to align their work or life pursuits with their deepest interests and values. By following your passion, you embark on a journey that is personally fulfilling and meaningful. It fuels your drive, ignites creativity, and enables you to make a lasting impact in your chosen field. Your passion becomes the guiding force that propels you forward, helping you overcome obstacles and find joy in your endeavors. When you follow your passion, you are more likely to experience a sense of purpose and fulfillment, as you are engaging in activities that resonate with your true self. It is through the pursuit of your passion that you can unlock your full potential and create a life that is uniquely yours.

FOLLOWING YOUR PASSION brings a sense of authenticity and alignment to your life. It allows you to tap into your natural talents and interests, leading to a greater sense of fulfillment and satisfaction. When you are engaged in activities that ignite your passion, work doesn't feel like a burden, but rather an enjoyable pursuit that brings you joy and fulfillment.

By following your passion, you are more likely to stay motivated and committed to your goals, even in the face of challenges and setbacks. Your passion acts as a driving force that propels you forward, helping you overcome obstacles and persevere in the pursuit of your dreams. It fuels your determination and resilience, enabling you to push beyond your limits and achieve extraordinary results.

Moreover, following your passion opens doors to personal growth and self-discovery. It encourages you to continuously learn, improve, and expand your skills in areas that genuinely interest you. The process of pursuing your passion allows you to uncover hidden talents, discover new possibilities, and embrace a journey of lifelong learning.

Additionally, when you follow your passion, you inspire others to do the same. Your enthusiasm, dedication, and authenticity serve as a source of inspiration for those around you. By pursuing your passion, you demonstrate the courage to live life on your own terms, encouraging others to do the same and create a ripple effect of passion-driven pursuits.

Ultimately, following your passion can lead to a life filled with meaning, fulfillment, and personal satisfaction. It allows you to make a positive impact on the world by bringing your unique talents and gifts to the forefront. So, listen to your inner calling, embrace your passions, and embark on a journey that aligns with who you truly are. By following your passion, you have the potential to create a life that is both personally rewarding and inspiring to others.

When you follow your passion, you experience a deep sense of fulfillment and a genuine connection to your work. It brings out your best self, as you are naturally inclined to invest time and effort into something that resonates with your inner desires and interests. This alignment between your passion and your pursuits creates a harmonious balance in your life, where work becomes a source of joy rather than a mere obligation.

Following your passion allows you to tap into your creative potential. It unleashes your imagination and encourages you to think outside the box, bringing fresh perspectives and innovative ideas to the forefront. The enthusiasm and energy that come from pursuing your passion fuel your creativity and enable you to make a unique and meaningful contribution to your chosen field.

Moreover, following your passion empowers you to overcome challenges and setbacks with resilience and determination. The love and enthusiasm you have for your work act as a powerful driving force, propelling you forward even in the face of adversity. It provides the motivation and strength to persevere, learn from failures, and adapt your approach to achieve your goals.

Following your passion also promotes a sense of authenticity and personal fulfillment. It allows you to live in alignment with your true values and aspirations, leading to a greater sense of self-fulfillment and happiness. When you are engaged in work that reflects your passions, you feel a deep sense of purpose and a strong connection to the impact you are making.

Furthermore, following your passion encourages continuous growth and personal development. As you delve deeper into your areas of interest, you naturally seek opportunities to expand your knowledge, skills, and expertise. This pursuit of mastery not only enhances your abilities but also opens doors to new opportunities and professional advancement.

It instills a sense of purpose, fulfillment, and genuine enthusiasm that radiates through your work, relationships, and overall well-being. It allows you to create a life that is aligned with your true self, where you wake up each day excited to pursue your passions and make a positive impact in the world.

Be Prepared for Criticism

Being prepared for criticism is a valuable lesson advocated by Mark Zuckerberg. It acknowledges the reality that when you put yourself out there and pursue your passions, you may encounter criticism and negative feedback from others. Here are further insights into the implications of being prepared for criticism:

Developing Resilience: Being prepared for criticism helps you develop resilience. Criticism can be disheartening and challenging to navigate, but by recognizing its potential existence, you can prepare yourself emotionally and mentally. Building resilience allows you to bounce back from criticism, learn from it, and continue progressing towards your goals.

Embracing Constructive Feedback: Not all criticism is negative. Being prepared for criticism enables you to discern between constructive feedback and baseless negativity. Constructive criticism can provide valuable insights, help you improve, and refine your work or approach. By embracing constructive feedback, you can grow and develop your skills.

Maintaining a Growth Mindset: Being open to criticism fosters a growth mindset. It encourages you to view criticism as an opportunity for growth and learning rather than a personal attack. By embracing feedback and seeing it as a chance to improve, you can approach challenges with a positive mindset and a willingness to continuously develop and evolve.

Strengthening Your Convictions: Criticism can test your beliefs and convictions. Being prepared for criticism allows you to stand firm in your values, goals, and passions. It enables you to have confidence in your decisions and stay true to your vision, even when faced with opposing viewpoints. By understanding that criticism is a part of the journey, you can maintain your focus and determination.

Learning to Filter Feedback: Not all criticism is valuable or constructive. Being prepared for criticism helps you develop the ability to filter and evaluate feedback effectively. You can discern between constructive feedback that aligns with your goals and opinions that are simply subjective or uninformed. This skill allows you to maintain a sense of self and stay true to your purpose.

Resisting the Fear of Failure: Criticism can evoke a fear of failure and the judgment of others. Being prepared for criticism helps you overcome this fear by realizing that criticism is a natural part of growth and progress. It empowers you to persevere despite setbacks, stay focused on your goals, and embrace the potential lessons that come with constructive criticism.

Harnessing Motivation: Criticism, when channeled appropriately, can fuel your motivation. Being prepared for criticism allows you to use negative feedback as a driving force to prove doubters wrong, overcome challenges, and achieve even greater success. Criticism can serve as a source of motivation and determination to excel in your pursuits.

By being prepared for criticism, you can navigate the ups and downs of your journey with a resilient mindset. It enables you to learn from feedback, maintain your focus, and use criticism as a catalyst for growth and improvement. Remember, the ability to handle criticism constructively is an essential skill in your personal and professional development.

Be Diligent

The verse "Do you see someone skilled in their work? They will serve before kings; they will not serve before officials of low rank" from Proverbs 22:29 highlights the importance of diligence and hard work. Although not directly attributed to Mark Zuckerberg, this verse reflects the principles he embodies and the mindset he encourages. Here are further insights into the implications of being diligent:

Commitment to Excellence: Diligence involves a steadfast commitment to excellence in your work. It means giving your best effort, going the extra mile, and striving for high standards. By consistently demonstrating diligence, you increase your chances of achieving success and standing out among your peers.

Perseverance in the Face of Challenges: Diligence helps you persevere in the face of challenges and setbacks. It implies a willingness to put in the necessary effort and determination to overcome obstacles that may arise along your journey. Diligence keeps you focused on your goals and motivates you to keep pushing forward, even when the path becomes difficult.

Professional Growth and Development: Diligence is essential for professional growth and development. It means continually seeking opportunities to improve your skills, expand your knowledge, and refine your craft. By being diligent, you demonstrate a commitment to lifelong learning and strive to become the best version of yourself in your chosen field.

Building Trust and Reliability: Diligence builds trust and reliability. When you consistently demonstrate diligence in your work, you establish a reputation as someone who can be relied upon to deliver quality results. Others trust your abilities and are more likely to seek your expertise and collaborate with you.

Taking Ownership and Responsibility: Diligence involves taking ownership and responsibility for your work. It means being accountable for your actions, meeting deadlines, and ensuring that your tasks are completed with precision and care. Diligence allows you to take pride in your work and take ownership of the outcomes.

Seizing Opportunities: Diligence helps you seize opportunities that come your way. By being diligent, you position yourself to recognize and capitalize on openings for growth, advancement, and new experiences. Diligence allows you to make the most of these opportunities and maximize your potential.

Achieving Long-Term Success: Diligence is often a key factor in achieving long-term success. It is a characteristic that sets successful individuals apart, as they are willing to put in the consistent effort and attention to detail required to achieve their goals. Diligence helps you build a strong foundation for sustained success and enables you to withstand the challenges that may arise on your journey.

While not directly connected to Mark Zuckerberg, the concept of diligence aligns with his emphasis on hard work, commitment to excellence, and perseverance. By embracing diligence, you can enhance your professional growth, build trust, seize opportunities, and achieve long-term success in your endeavors. Remember, diligence is a key virtue that can help you reach your full potential and make a meaningful impact in your chosen field.

Don't be Afraid to Compete with the Giants

"Don't be afraid to compete with the giants" reflects Mark Zuckerberg's belief in challenging established norms and going up against formidable competitors. While not directly attributed to him, this mindset aligns with his entrepreneurial spirit and willingness to take on significant challenges. Here are further insights into the implications of not being afraid to compete with the giants:

Embracing Innovation: Competing with giants requires an innovative mindset. It involves thinking differently, identifying gaps in the market, and finding unique approaches to solving problems. By challenging established players, you can bring fresh ideas and disruptive innovations to the table.

Leveraging Differentiation: Competing with giants often involves finding your unique value proposition. Rather than trying to replicate what others are already doing, focus on what sets you apart. Differentiate yourself through unique features, exceptional customer service, or a specialized niche. Find ways to stand out from the crowd and offer something distinct.

Seizing Opportunities: Competing with giants can present significant opportunities. While established players may have a strong market presence, they might also have limitations or blind spots. By identifying and capitalizing on these opportunities, you can carve out your own space and gain a competitive advantage.

Disrupting the Status Quo: Competing with giants often involves disrupting traditional industries or business models. Don't be afraid to challenge the status quo and offer alternative solutions. By doing so, you can create new markets, redefine existing ones, and revolutionize industries.

Agility and Adaptability: Competing with giants requires agility and adaptability. Large companies may have more resources, but they can also be slower to adapt to changing market dynamics. By being nimble and responsive to customer needs, you can outmaneuver bigger competitors and seize opportunities more quickly.

Building a Strong Value Proposition: Competing with giants requires building a strong value proposition that resonates with customers. Focus on delivering exceptional products, services, or experiences that provide tangible benefits to your target audience. By consistently delivering value, you can attract customers and establish a loyal following.

Persistence and Resilience: Competing with giants is not without challenges. It requires persistence and resilience in the face of adversity. Be prepared to face setbacks and learn from them. Stay focused on your goals, adapt as needed, and remain determined to overcome obstacles along the way.

By embracing the mindset of not being afraid to compete with the giants, you can challenge the status quo, drive innovation, and carve out your own path to success. Remember, the size of your competition doesn't determine your potential for success. With the right strategy, differentiation, and persistence, you can make a significant impact and thrive in even the most competitive industries.

Be Focused

"Be focused" encapsulates Mark Zuckerberg's emphasis on maintaining a clear direction and unwavering attention to achieving your goals. While not directly attributed to him, this principle aligns with his entrepreneurial mindset and the disciplined approach he has demonstrated throughout his career. Here are further insights into the implications of being focused:

Clarity of Purpose: Being focused means having a clear sense of purpose and direction. It involves identifying your goals, understanding what you want to achieve, and aligning your actions with your overarching vision. By defining your purpose, you can prioritize your efforts and make intentional decisions that move you closer to your desired outcomes.

Eliminating Distractions: Being focused requires eliminating distractions that can hinder progress. It involves minimizing time-wasting activities, setting boundaries, and creating an environment conducive to concentration. By managing distractions effectively, you can maximize your productivity and stay on track towards your goals.

Concentrated Effort: Being focused entails dedicating concentrated effort to the task at hand. It means giving your full attention, energy, and resources to the most important priorities. By focusing on key activities and leveraging your strengths, you can achieve higher levels of performance and make significant progress towards your objectives.

Effective Time Management: Being focused necessitates effective time management. It involves prioritizing tasks, allocating time wisely, and avoiding multitasking. By optimizing your time and resources, you can allocate sufficient attention and energy to each activity, ensuring that you make the most of your available resources.

Resisting Shiny Object Syndrome: Being focused requires resisting the allure of shiny object syndrome, which refers to the temptation to constantly pursue new ideas or opportunities without staying committed to a particular path. By staying focused on your chosen direction, you can avoid distractions and maintain the discipline needed to see your initiatives through to completion.

Making Informed Decisions: Being focused allows for making informed decisions that align with your long-term goals. It entails considering the potential impact of each choice on your overall vision and strategically selecting the options that contribute to your desired outcomes. By making decisions with focus and purpose, you can create a pathway that leads to success.

Achieving Mastery: Being focused enables you to achieve mastery in your chosen field or area of interest. It involves dedicating the necessary time and effort to develop deep expertise, continuously learn and grow, and refine your skills. By immersing yourself in focused practice and deliberate learning, you can become an expert in your domain.

By embracing the principle of being focused, you can maximize your effectiveness, overcome distractions, and make significant progress towards your goals. Remember, a focused mindset allows you to channel your energy, resources, and attention towards the most meaningful pursuits, leading to increased productivity, personal growth, and long-term success.

Learn to Take Risks

"Learn to take risks" reflects Mark Zuckerberg's willingness to embrace uncertainty and step outside of comfort zones in pursuit of innovation and growth. While not directly attributed to him, this principle aligns with his entrepreneurial spirit and his bold decision-making. Here are further insights into the implications of learning to take risks:

Embracing Growth and Innovation: Taking risks is often essential for driving growth and fostering innovation. It involves pushing boundaries, exploring uncharted territory, and challenging conventional thinking. By embracing calculated risks, you open yourself up to new possibilities and opportunities for creative breakthroughs.

Overcoming Fear of Failure: Learning to take risks involves overcoming the fear of failure. It means understanding that setbacks and mistakes are part of the learning process. By reframing failure as a valuable learning experience, you can develop resilience, learn from your mistakes, and continue moving forward towards your goals.

Seizing Opportunities: Taking risks allows you to seize opportunities that come your way. It involves recognizing potential gains and benefits that may arise from stepping into the unknown. By being open to new possibilities, you can capitalize on opportunities for personal and professional growth that may have otherwise been missed.

Fostering Adaptability: Taking risks encourages adaptability in the face of uncertainty. It requires being flexible, willing to adjust your strategies, and embrace change. By learning to adapt to new situations, you can navigate shifting landscapes and position yourself for success in dynamic environments.

Building Resilience: Taking risks builds resilience, as it often involves encountering challenges and setbacks along the way. By facing adversity and learning to persevere, you develop a stronger capacity to bounce back and maintain focus despite obstacles. Resilience helps you stay motivated and committed to your goals.

Stretching Your Limits: Taking risks enables you to stretch your limits and discover your true potential. It involves stepping outside of your comfort zone and pushing yourself beyond familiar boundaries. By challenging yourself and embracing discomfort, you can uncover hidden strengths and capabilities.

Creating Opportunities for Success: Learning to take risks creates opportunities for success that may not have existed otherwise. It involves taking calculated chances, pursuing unconventional paths, and positioning yourself for breakthrough moments. By venturing into undiscoverd territory, you increase your potential for significant achievements and remarkable outcomes.

By adopting a mindset of learning to take risks, you can unlock new possibilities, foster innovation, and achieve personal and professional growth. Remember, calculated risks, combined with thoughtful analysis and a willingness to learn from both successes and failures, can lead to transformative experiences and propel you towards achieving extraordinary results.

Stick to the Process

"Stick to the process" reflects Mark Zuckerberg's emphasis on the importance of following a systematic approach or methodology in achieving success. While not directly attributed to him, this principle aligns with his disciplined mindset and his focus on long-term strategies. Here are further insights into the implications of sticking to the process:

Consistency and Discipline: Sticking to the process requires consistency and discipline in your actions. It involves committing to a set of guidelines, routines, or steps that contribute to your progress. By adhering to a structured approach, you can establish a sense of stability, maintain focus, and avoid distractions that may derail your efforts.

Clear Goal Orientation: Sticking to the process keeps you focused on your goals. It involves aligning your actions with the desired outcomes and consistently working towards achieving them. By adhering to a well-defined process, you can track your progress, make adjustments as necessary, and stay on track towards your objectives.

Overcoming Short-Term Obstacles: The process often entails encountering short-term obstacles or challenges. By sticking to the process, you maintain a long-term perspective, understanding that temporary setbacks should not derail your overall progress. It allows you to persevere through difficulties and navigate hurdles with resilience and determination.

Building Incremental Progress: Sticking to the process emphasizes the importance of incremental progress. It recognizes that significant achievements are often the result of consistent, small steps taken over time. By following a systematic approach, you can break down larger goals into manageable tasks, focus on incremental improvements, and build momentum towards your desired outcomes.

Trusting in the Methodology: Sticking to the process involves trusting in the methodology or strategy you have established. It acknowledges that the chosen approach has been thoughtfully designed and has proven effectiveness. By having confidence in the process, you can avoid unnecessary second-guessing and remain committed to your chosen path.

Resisting Impulsive Decisions: Sticking to the process helps you resist impulsive decisions or actions that may lead to suboptimal outcomes. It encourages thoughtful evaluation, data-driven analysis, and a strategic mindset. By following the process, you can make informed decisions based on evidence and avoid being swayed by short-term fluctuations or emotions.

Achieving Long-Term Success: Sticking to the process lays the foundation for long-term success. It recognizes that sustained effort, guided by a well-defined process, can lead to significant accomplishments over time. By maintaining consistency, discipline, and focus, you increase your chances of achieving your goals and realizing long-term success.

By embracing the principle of sticking to the process, you can maintain focus, navigate obstacles, and achieve your desired outcomes. Remember, success often stems from a well-defined and systematic approach, and by adhering to the process, you position yourself for long-term growth and sustainable results.

SUMMARY

In this captivating book, we delve into the success strategies of some of the world's most influential men: Bill Gates, Elon Musk, Robert Kiyosaki, Warren Buffett, Steve Jobs, and Mark Zuckerberg. Through their stories and philosophies, we uncover the underlying principles and actionable steps that have propelled them to extraordinary heights of success.

Each of these exceptional individuals has made a profound impact in their respective fields, from technology and entrepreneurship to investing and innovation. By studying their strategies, we can glean valuable insights and practical wisdom that can be applied to our own lives.

From the relentless determination of Bill Gates to the audacious risk-taking of Elon Musk, and the investment wisdom of Warren Buffett, we learn the importance of perseverance, calculated risk, and long-term thinking. We also discover the passion-driven approach of Steve Jobs and the relentless pursuit of innovation demonstrated by Mark Zuckerberg.

But this book is not limited to admiration alone. We go beyond inspiration and distill their strategies into actionable steps that can be incorporated into our own lives. Whether aspiring to become an entrepreneur, investor, or leader, this guide equips us with the tools, mindset, and strategies to turn our dreams into reality.

By embracing the success strategies of these remarkable individuals, we have the opportunity to unleash our full potential, redefine our own versions of success, and embark on a transformative journey towards personal and professional greatness. It's time to learn from the world's most successful men and apply their wisdom to create a life of limitless possibilities.

CONCLUSION

In conclusion, the success strategies of the world's most influential men, including Bill Gates, Elon Musk, Robert Kiyosaki, Warren Buffett, Steve Jobs, and Mark Zuckerberg, provide us with invaluable insights and practical wisdom to guide our own paths to success.

Throughout this book, we have learned that success is not a result of luck or chance, but a deliberate combination of mindset, dedication, and strategic action. Each of these extraordinary individuals has demonstrated a unique approach to achieving greatness in their respective fields, leaving an indelible mark on the world.

From Bill Gates' relentless work ethic and strategic thinking to Elon Musk's audacity and innovation, we see the power of pushing boundaries and embracing calculated risks. Robert Kiyosaki's financial intelligence and Warren Buffett's patient, value-based investing remind us of the importance of building wealth and making informed decisions.

Steve Jobs' emphasis on passion, focus, and perfection in design inspires us to pursue our true passions, while Mark Zuckerberg's fearlessness, resilience, and ability to adapt encourage us to stay nimble in an ever-changing world.

But the journey doesn't end with inspiration alone. It is through the application of these success strategies in our own lives that we can truly transform and achieve our greatest aspirations. By embodying the dedication, resilience, and innovative thinking of these remarkable individuals, we have the power to create our own path to success.

Remember, success is a personal journey, and each of us has the potential to define what it means to us. By integrating the lessons learned from these successful men, we can unleash our full potential, overcome obstacles, and make a lasting impact in our chosen fields.

So, let us embrace the lessons shared by these visionaries, chart our own course, and embark on a journey of personal and professional growth. The success strategies of Bill Gates, Elon Musk, Robert Kiyosaki, Warren Buffett, Steve Jobs, and Mark Zuckerberg serve as beacons of inspiration and guidance, lighting our path towards a future of limitless possibilities and unparalleled success. It is up to us to seize the knowledge gained and turn it into action. The world is waiting for our unique contributions, and now is the time to make our mark.

Don't miss out!

Visit the website below and you can sign up to receive emails whenever GORDON MILLS publishes a new book. There's no charge and no obligation.

https://books2read.com/r/B-A-CZEZ-UEJLC

BOOKS 2 READ

Connecting independent readers to independent writers.

Also by GORDON MILLS

5 Ways to Become Mysterious

Building Generational Wealth : Unveiling the Secrets of Long-Term Financial Prosperity

The 5 Rules of Billionaires

The 4 Strategic Secrets of Success : Unlocking Your Success Blueprint - Secrets to Extraordinary Achievement

The 5 Rules of Money : The Golden Rules of Making and Increasing Money

The 7cs of Success : Confidence, Consistency, Conception, Concentration, Character, Commitment and Capacity to Enjoy Success Strategies of the World Most Successful men and how to Apply them in Your Life

Milton Keynes UK
Ingram Content Group UK Ltd.
UKHW010711040923
428018UK00014B/873